FIRST PAST THE POST®

Mathematics: Practice Papers

Multiple Choice Book 2

© 2019 ElevenPlusExams.co.uk   COPYING STRICTLY PROHIBITED

How to use this book to make the most of 11 plus exam preparation

It is important to remember that for 11 plus exams there is no national syllabus, no pass mark and no retake option. It is therefore vital that your child is fully primed to perform to the best of their ability so that they give themselves the best possible chance on the day.

Unlike similar publications, the **First Past The Post®** series uniquely assesses your child's performance on a question-by-question basis, helping to identify areas for improvement and providing suggestions for further targeted tests. By entering the unique Peer-Compare™ access code for this book on our website, your child's performance can be compared anonymously to that of others who have taken the same tests.

Mathematics: Practice Papers

This collection of four timed tests is representative of the standard Mathematics section of contemporary multi-discipline 11 plus and Common Entrance exams. Each test contains 50 questions and is designed to be completed in 50 minutes. This time is based on classroom testing sessions held at our centre. These tests are especially representative of the Granada Learning (GL) Mathematics papers, but provide useful practice for all exam boards.

Never has it been more useful to learn from mistakes!

Students can improve by as much as 15%, not only by focused practice, but also by targeting any weak areas.

How to manage your child's practice

To get the most up-to-date information, visit our website, www.elevenplusexams.co.uk, the UK's largest online resource for 11 plus, with over 65,000 webpages and a forum administered by a select group of experienced moderators.

About the authors

The Eleven Plus Exams' **First Past The Post®** series has been created by a team of experienced tutors and authors from leading British universities.

Published by Technical One Ltd t/a Eleven Plus Exams

With special thanks to all the children who tested our material at the ElevenPlusExams centre in Harrow.

ISBN: 978-1-912364-49-7

Copyright © ElevenPlusExams.co.uk 2019

All rights reserved. No part of this publication may be reproduced, stored or introduced into a retrieval system or transmitted in any form or by any means, without the prior written permission of the publisher nor may be circulated in any form of binding or cover other than the one in which it was published and without a similar condition including this condition being imposed on the subsequent publisher.

About Us

At Eleven Plus Exams, we supply high-quality 11 plus tuition for your children. Our free website at **www.elevenplusexams.co.uk** is the largest website in the UK that specifically prepares children for the 11 plus exams. We also provide online services to schools and our **First Past The Post®** range of books has been well-received by schools, tuition centres and parents.

Eleven Plus Exams is recognised as a trusted and authoritative source. We have been quoted in numerous national newspapers, including *The Telegraph*, *The Observer*, the *Daily Mail* and *The Sunday Telegraph*, as well as on national television (BBC1 and Channel 4), and BBC radio.

Our website offers a vast amount of information and advice on the 11 plus, including a moderated online forum, books, downloadable material and online services to enhance your child's chances of success. Set up in 2004, the website grew from an initial 20 webpages to more than 65,000 today, and has been visited by millions of parents. It is moderated by experts in the field, who provide support for parents both before and after the exams.

Don't forget to visit **www.elevenplusexams.co.uk** and see why we are the market's leading one-stop shop for all your 11 plus needs. You will find:

- ✓ Comprehensive quality content and advice written by 11 plus experts
- ✓ Eleven Plus Exams online shop supplying a wide range of practice books, e-papers, software and apps
- ✓ Lots of FREE practice papers to download
- ✓ Professional tuition service
- ✓ Short revision courses
- ✓ Year-long 11 plus courses
- ✓ Mock exams tailored to reflect those of the main examining bodies

Other Titles in the First Past The Post® Series
11+ Essentials Range of Books

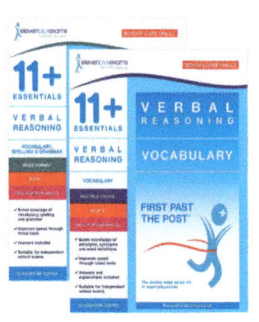

978-1-912364-60-2	Verbal Reasoning: Cloze Tests Book 1 - Mixed Format
978-1-912364-61-9	Verbal Reasoning: Cloze Tests Book 2 - Mixed Format
978-1-912364-78-7	Verbal Reasoning: Cloze Tests Book 3 - Mixed Format
978-1-912364-79-4	Verbal Reasoning: Cloze Tests Book 4 - Mixed Format
978-1-912364-62-6	Verbal Reasoning: Vocabulary Book 1 - Multiple Choice
978-1-912364-63-3	Verbal Reasoning: Vocabulary Book 2 - Multiple Choice
978-1-912364-64-0	Verbal Reasoning: Vocabulary Book 3 - Multiple Choice
978-1-912364-65-7	Verbal Reasoning: Vocabulary, Spelling and Grammar Book 1 - Multiple Choice
978-1-912364-66-4	Verbal Reasoning: Vocabulary, Spelling and Grammar Book 2 - Multiple Choice
978-1-912364-68-8	Verbal Reasoning: Vocabulary in Context Level 1
978-1-912364-69-5	Verbal Reasoning: Vocabulary in Context Level 2
978-1-912364-70-1	Verbal Reasoning: Vocabulary in Context Level 3
978-1-912364-71-8	Verbal Reasoning: Vocabulary in Context Level 4
978-1-912364-74-9	Verbal Reasoning: Vocabulary Puzzles Book 1
978-1-912364-75-6	Verbal Reasoning: Vocabulary Puzzles Book 2
978-1-912364-76-3	Verbal Reasoning: Practice Papers Book 1 - Multiple Choice

978-1-912364-02-2	English: Comprehensions Classic Literature Book 1 - Multiple Choice
978-1-912364-05-3	English: Comprehensions Contemporary Literature Book 1 - Multiple Choice
978-1-912364-08-4	English: Comprehensions Non-Fiction Book 1 - Multiple Choice
978-1-912364-14-5	English: Mini Comprehensions - Inference Book 1
978-1-912364-15-2	English: Mini Comprehensions - Inference Book 2
978-1-912364-16-9	English: Mini Comprehensions - Inference Book 3
978-1-912364-11-4	English: Mini Comprehensions - Fact-Finding Book 1
978-1-912364-12-1	English: Mini Comprehensions - Fact-Finding Book 2
978-1-912364-21-3	English: Spelling, Punctuation and Grammar Book 1
978-1-912364-00-8	English: Practice Papers Book 1 - Multiple Choice
978-1-912364-17-6	Creative Writing Examples

978-1-912364-30-5	Numerical Reasoning: Quick-Fire Book 1
978-1-912364-31-2	Numerical Reasoning: Quick-Fire Book 2
978-1-912364-32-9	Numerical Reasoning: Quick-Fire Book 1 - Multiple Choice
978-1-912364-33-6	Numerical Reasoning: Quick-Fire Book 2 - Multiple Choice
978-1-912364-34-3	Numerical Reasoning: Multi-Part Book 1
978-1-912364-35-0	Numerical Reasoning: Multi-Part Book 2
978-1-912364-36-7	Numerical Reasoning: Multi-Part Book 1 - Multiple Choice
978-1-912364-37-4	Numerical Reasoning: Multi-Part Book 2 - Multiple Choice

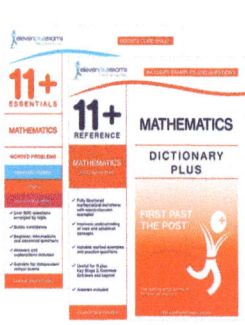

978-1-912364-43-5	Mathematics: Mental Arithmetic Book 1
978-1-912364-44-2	Mathematics: Mental Arithmetic Book 2
978-1-912364-45-9	Mathematics: Worded Problems Book 1
978-1-912364-46-6	Mathematics: Worded Problems Book 2
978-1-912364-52-7	Mathematics: Worded Problems Book 3
978-1-912364-47-3	Mathematics: Dictionary Plus
978-1-912364-50-3	Mathematics: Crossword Puzzles Book 1
978-1-912364-51-0	Mathematics: Crossword Puzzles Book 2
978-1-912364-48-0	Mathematics: Practice Papers Book 1 - Multiple Choice

978-1-912364-87-9	Non-Verbal Reasoning: 2D Book 1 - Multiple Choice
978-1-912364-88-6	Non-Verbal Reasoning: 2D Book 2 - Multiple Choice
978-1-912364-85-5	Non-Verbal Reasoning: 3D Book 1 - Multiple Choice
978-1-912364-86-2	Non-Verbal Reasoning: 3D Book 2 - Multiple Choice
978-1-912364-83-1	Non-Verbal Reasoning: Practice Papers Book 1 - Multiple Choice

Contents

Glossary	vi
Test A	1
Test B	9
Test C	17
Test D	25
Answer Sheets	33
Answers & Explanations	43
Peer-Compare™ access code	inside front cover

This book comprises four tests, made up of 50 questions each.
Each test should be completed in 50 minutes.

Glossary

Learn the meanings of the terms listed below to expand your mathematical vocabulary.

Apothem - a line segment from the centre of a regular polygon to the midpoint of one of its sides.
Bearing - an angle given in three figures that is measured clockwise from the north direction, e.g. 025°.
BIDMAS - an acronym for **B**rackets, **I**ndices, **D**ivision and **M**ultiplication, and **A**ddition and **S**ubtraction. It is the agreed order of operations used to clarify which should be performed first in a given expression.
Bimodal - when a collection of data has two modes, e.g. in the dataset: {1, 1, 1, 2, 4, 5, 5, 5}, the two modes are 1 and 5.
Bisect - to divide into two equal parts.
Coefficient - a constant that is placed before a variable in an algebraic expression, e.g. in the term $4x$, the coefficient is 4.
Complementary angles - two angles are complementary if they add up to 90°.
Cube number - a number that can be produced by multiplying another number by itself twice, e.g. 8 (= 2 x 2 x 2).
Edge - a line segment that joins two vertices of a 2D shape, or a line segment at which two faces meet in a 3D shape.
Enlargement - a type of transformation in which the size of an object is changed, whilst the ratio of the lengths of its sides stays the same.
Equidistant - two or more points are equidistant if they are the same distance from a common point.
Face - an individual surface of a 3D shape.
Fair - free from bias or equally likely to occur.
Gallon - a unit of volume used for measuring liquids. It is equal to 8 pints, or 4.55 litres.
Gradient - a measure of the steepness of a straight line.
Highest common factor (HCF) - the largest number that is a factor of two or more given numbers, e.g. 5 is the highest common factor of 10 and 15.
Imperial units - the system of units first defined in the British Weights and Measures Act. These units are no longer officially used in Britain, e.g. inches, feet, pints etc.
Inscribe - to draw a shape within another so that their edges touch, but do not intersect.
Integer - a whole number, i.e. not a decimal or a fraction.
Isosceles trapezium - a trapezium with one line of symmetry, two pairs of equal angles and one pair of parallel sides.
Leap year - a calendar year that occurs every four years. It has 366 days, instead of 365, and includes the 29th February. The year 2012 was a leap year.
Lowest common multiple (LCM) - the smallest number that is a multiple of two or more given numbers, e.g. 6 is the lowest common multiple of 2 and 3.
Metric units - a system of units based on multiples of 10, e.g. millimetre (mm), centimetre (cm) or metre (m).
Net - a 2D pattern that can be cut out and folded to make a 3D shape.
Parallel - lines that run side-by-side, always remain the same distance apart and never intersect, even if they are extended.
Perimeter - the total distance around the outside of a 2D shape.
Perpendicular - two lines are perpendicular if they are at an angle of 90° to each other.
Polygon - a 2D shape with three or more straight sides and no curved sides, e.g. triangle, pentagon, hexagon.
Polyhedron - a 3D shape whose faces are polygons, e.g. triangular pyramid, octahedron.
Prime factor - one of a collection of prime numbers whose product is a particular number, i.e. 2 x 2 x 3 = 12, so 2, 2 and 3 are the prime factors of 12.
Prime number - an integer greater than 1 that has no factors other than 1 and itself, e.g. 2, 3, 5.
Prism - a solid 3D shape with two identical, parallel end faces that are connected by flat sides.
Pyramid - a solid 3D shape whose base is a polygon and has triangular faces that meet at a single vertex.
Quadrilateral - a 2D shape with four straight sides. Quadrilaterals are polygons.
Reflective symmetry - a shape or an object has reflective symmetry if an imaginary line can be drawn that divides the shape into two, so that one half is a reflection of the other in the imaginary line.
Regular - a regular polygon has sides of equal length.
Remainder - a number that is left over after a division.
Rotational symmetry - a shape or an object has rotational symmetry if it can be rotated, but still appears to be in the same original position, e.g. a square has rotational symmetry of order four, because it can be rotated four times, but still appears the same.
Scalene - the sides of a scalene triangle are all of different lengths.
Sequence - a list of numbers or objects arranged in a particular order, which is defined by a specific rule, or set of rules.
Square number - a number that can be produced by multiplying another number by itself, e.g. 16 (= 4 x 4).
Supplementary angles - two angles are supplementary if they add up to 180°.
Triangle - a 2D shape with three straight sides. Triangles are polygons.
Triangular number - a number that can be represented by a group of equally spaced points arranged in a triangle, e.g. 1, 3, 6:
Vertex - a point at which two or more straight lines meet.

Place Value

The numerical value of a digit in a number.
For example, in the number 1234.567, the digit 3 has a place value of tens.

1	2	3	4	.	5	6	7
thousands	hundreds	tens	units	decimal point	tenths	hundredths	thousandths

Special Numbers

	1st	2nd	3rd	4th	5th	6th	7th	8th	9th	10th	11th	12th	13th	14th	15th	16th	17th	18th	19th	20th
Even	2	4	6	8	10	12	14	16	18	20	22	24	26	28	30	32	34	36	38	40
Odd	1	3	5	7	9	11	13	15	17	19	21	23	25	27	29	31	33	35	37	39
Square	1	4	9	16	25	36	49	64	81	100	121	144	169	196	225	256	289	324	361	400
Cube	1	8	27	64	125	216	343	512	729	1000	1331	1728	2197	2744	3375	4096	4913	5832	6859	8000
Triangular	1	3	6	10	15	21	28	36	45	55	66	78	91	105	120	136	153	171	190	210
Prime	2	3	5	7	11	13	17	19	23	29	31	37	41	43	47	53	59	61	67	71
Fibonacci	1	1	2	3	5	8	13	21	34	55	89	144	233	377	610	987	1597	2584	4181	6765

Equivalent Decimals, Fractions & Percentages

Percentage	5%	10%	15%	20%	25%	30%	35%	40%	45%	50%	55%	60%	65%	70%	75%	80%	85%	90%	95%	100%	150%
Fraction	$1/20$	$1/10$	$3/20$	$1/5$	$1/4$	$3/10$	$7/20$	$2/5$	$9/20$	$1/2$	$11/20$	$3/5$	$13/20$	$7/10$	$3/4$	$4/5$	$17/20$	$9/10$	$19/20$	$1/1$	$3/2$
Decimal	0.05	0.1	0.15	0.2	0.25	0.3	0.35	0.4	0.45	0.5	0.55	0.6	0.65	0.7	0.75	0.8	0.85	0.9	0.95	1	1.5

Mathematical Symbols

+	addition
−	subtraction
×	multiplication
÷	Division
±	positive or negative
=	equals
<	less than
>	greater than
≈	approximately equal to
≤	less than or equal to
≥	greater than or equal to
≠	not equal to
a^2	squared number
a^3	cubed number
%	percentage
$\sqrt{a}$	square root
$\sqrt[3]{a}$	cubed root
$\dot{a}$	recurring number
$a : b$	ratio
$a°$	degrees
$\bar{a}$	mean
(x, y)	coordinates
⌐	right angle
$\binom{x}{y}$	column vector (column matrix)
a/b	fraction
$\{a, b\}$	dataset
π	pi

Equivalent Periods of Time

1 minute	60 seconds
1 hour	60 minutes
1 day	24 hours
1 week	7 days
1 year	12 months (365 days)
1 leap year	366 days
1 decade	10 years
1 century	100 years
1 millennium	1,000 years

Roman Numerals

When a symbol appears *after* a numerically larger symbol, their values are added. When a symbol appears *before* a numerically larger symbol, their values are subtracted.

1	I
2	II
3	III
4	IV
5	**V**
6	VI
7	VII
8	VIII
9	IX
10	**X**
20	XX
30	XXX

40	XL
50	**L**
60	LX
70	LXX
80	LXXX
90	XC
100	**C**
200	CC
300	CCC
400	CD
500	**D**
1,000	**M**

Time Conversion

24-hour clock	12-hour clock
00:00	12.00am
01:00	1.00am
02:00	2.00am
03:00	3.00am
04:00	4.00am
05:00	5.00am
06:00	6.00am
07:00	7.00am
08:00	8.00am
09:00	9.00am
10:00	10.00am
11:00	11.00am
12:00	12.00pm
13:00	1.00pm
14:00	2.00pm
15:00	3.00pm
16:00	4.00pm
17:00	5.00pm
18:00	6.00pm
19:00	7.00pm
20:00	8.00pm
21:00	9.00pm
22:00	10.00pm
23:00	11.00pm

Units of Measurement

	Metric system		Imperial system		
	Units	Conversion	Units	Conversion	Metric approximation
Mass	milligramme (mg)	1mg = 0.1cg = 0.001g	ounce (oz)	1oz = $^1/_{16}$ lb	1oz ≈ 28g
	centigramme (cg)	1cg = 10mg = 0.01g	pound (lb)	1lb = 16oz	1lb ≈ 0.45kg
	gramme (g)	1g = 100cg = 0.001kg	stone (st)	1st = 14lb	1st ≈ 6kg
	kilogramme (kg)	1kg = 1,000g = 0.001t	ton	1 ton = 160st	1 ton ≈ 0.91 tonne
	tonne (t)	1t = 1,000,000g = 1,000kg			
Length	millimetre (mm)	1mm = 0.1cm = 0.001m	inch (in or ")	1in = $^1/_{12}$ ft	1in ≈ 25mm
	centimetre (cm)	1cm = 10mm = 0.01m	foot (ft or ')	1ft = 12in	1ft ≈ 30cm
	metre (m)	1m = 100cm = 0.001km	yard (yd)	1yd = 3ft	1yd ≈ 91cm
	kilometre (km)	1km = 100,000cm = 1,000m	mile	1 mile = 1,760yd	1 mile ≈ 1.6km
Volume	millilitre (ml)	1ml = 0.1cl = 0.001l = 1cm³	fluid ounce (fl. oz)	1fl. oz = $^1/_{20}$ pt	1fl. oz ≈ 28ml
	centilitre (cl)	1cl = 10ml = 0.01l = 10cm³	pint (pt)	1pt = 20fl. oz	1pt ≈ 0.57l
	litre (l)	1l = 100cl = 0.001kl = 1,000cm³	gallon (gal)	1gal = 8pt	1gal ≈ 4.5l
	kilolitre (kl)	1kl = 1,000l = 1,000,000cm³			

Types of Angles

Zero angle
Equivalent to 0°

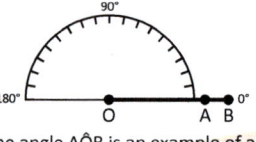

The angle AÔB is an example of a zero angle.

Acute angle
An angle greater than 0°, but smaller than 90°

Angle $c°$ (AÔB) is an example of an acute angle.

Right angle
An angle of 90°

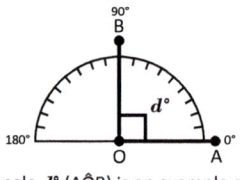

Angle $d°$ (AÔB) is an example of a right angle.

Obtuse angle
An angle greater than 90°, but smaller than 180°

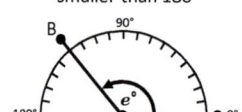

Angle $e°$ (AÔB) is an example of an obtuse angle.

Flat angle
An angle of 180°

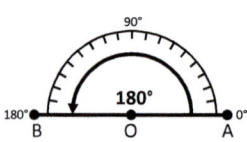

The angle AÔB is an example of a flat angle.

Reflex angle
An angle greater than 180°, but smaller than 360°

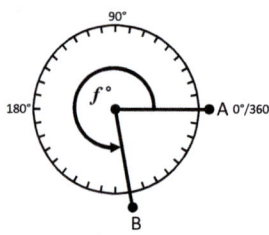

Angle $f°$ (AÔB) is an example of a reflex angle.

Full rotation
A full turn, equal to 360°

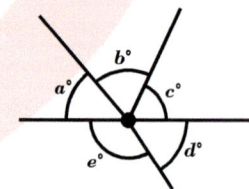

Pairs of Angles

Alternate angles
Alternate angles are formed when a straight line crosses a set of parallel lines.

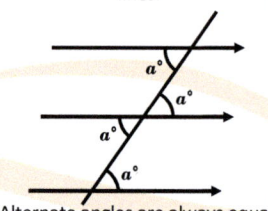

Alternate angles are always equal.

Corresponding angles
Corresponding angles are formed when a straight line crosses a set of parallel lines.

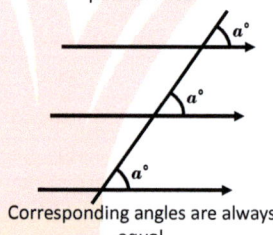

Corresponding angles are always equal.

Complementary angles
Two angles that add up to 90°

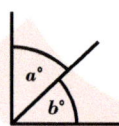 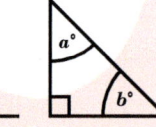

Since $a° + b° = 90°$, they are complementary angles.

Supplementary angles
Two angles that add up to 180°

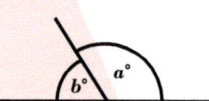

Since $a° + b° = 180°$, they are supplementary angles.

Opposite angles
Angles that are opposite each other when two lines intersect

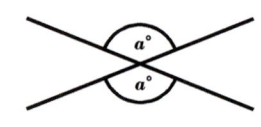

Opposite angles are always equal.

Angles in a revolution
The angles formed when lines meet each other at a point, or intersect

All the angles in a revolution always add up to 360°. Here, $a° + b° + c° + d° + e° = 360°$.

2D Shapes

Figures with two dimensions: length and width.

Circle	Right-angled triangle	Equilateral triangle	Isosceles triangle	Scalene triangle
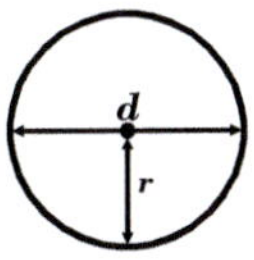 r = radius d = diameter The perimeter of a circle is its circumference.	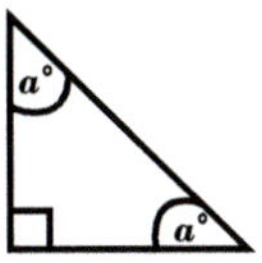 One angle is a right angle (90°). The other two angles are complementary.	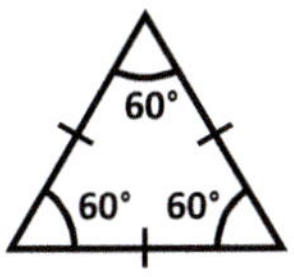 All three angles are equal (60°). All three sides are of equal length.	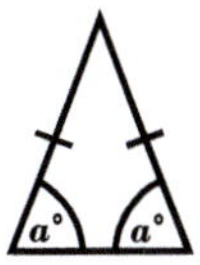 Two angles are equal. Two sides are of equal length.	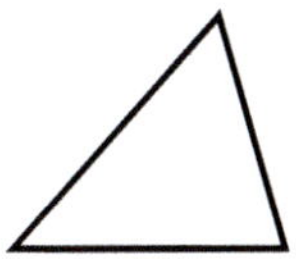 No angles are equal. No sides are of equal length.
Square	**Trapezium**	**Rhombus**	**Parallelogram**	**Kite**
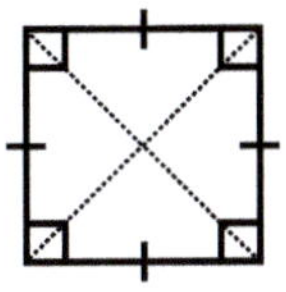 All four angles are equal (90°). All four sides are of equal length. The diagonals bisect each other at 90°.	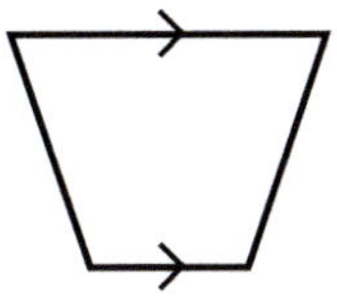 One pair of opposite sides is parallel.	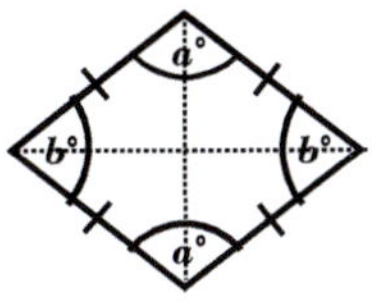 Opposite angles are equal. All sides are of equal length. The diagonals bisect each other at 90°.	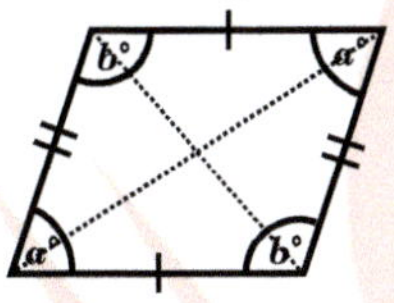 Opposite angles are equal. Opposite sides are parallel and of equal length. The diagonals bisect each other.	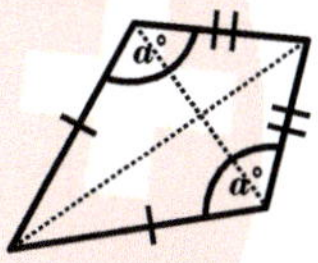 Two of the opposite angles are equal. Two pairs of sides are of equal lengths. The diagonals intersect at 90°.
Regular pentagon	**Regular hexagon**	**Regular heptagon**	**Regular octagon**	**Regular nonagon**
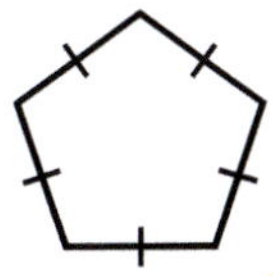 All five angles are equal. All five sides are of equal length. The sum of the interior angles is 540°.	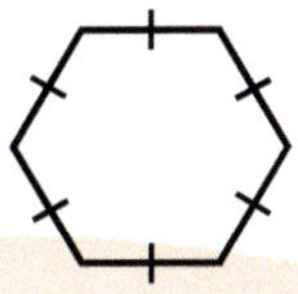 All six angles are equal. All six sides are of equal length. The sum of the interior angles is 720°.	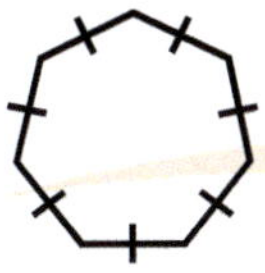 All seven angles are equal. All seven sides are of equal length. The sum of the interior angles is 900°.	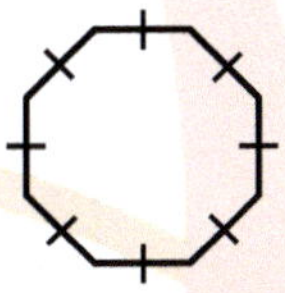 All eight angles are equal. All eight sides are of equal length. The sum of the interior angles is 1,080°.	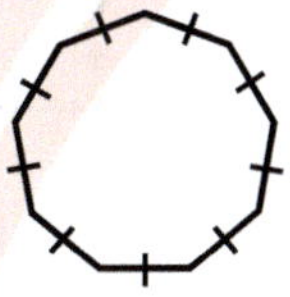 All nine angles are equal. All nine sides are of equal length. The sum of the interior angles is 1,260°.

3D Shapes

Figures with three dimensions: length, width and depth.

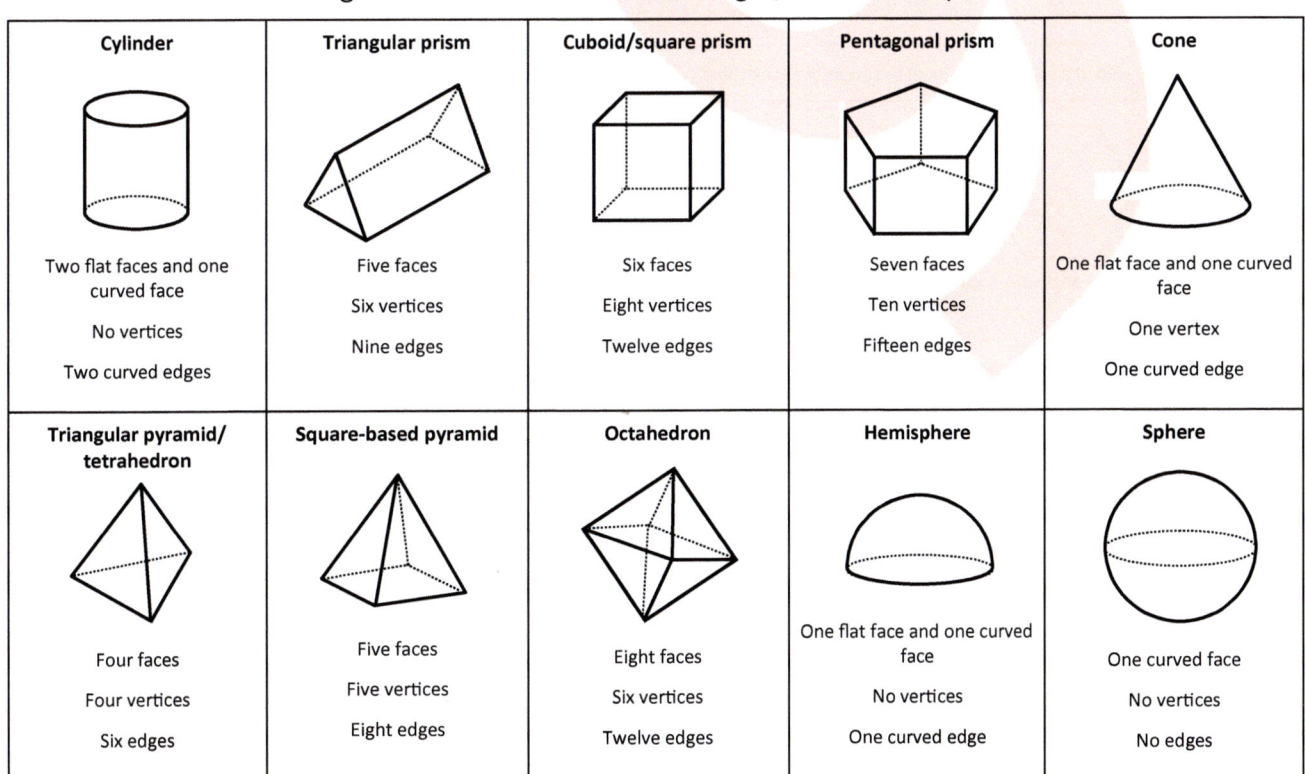

Cylinder	Triangular prism	Cuboid/square prism	Pentagonal prism	Cone
Two flat faces and one curved face No vertices Two curved edges	Five faces Six vertices Nine edges	Six faces Eight vertices Twelve edges	Seven faces Ten vertices Fifteen edges	One flat face and one curved face One vertex One curved edge
Triangular pyramid/ tetrahedron	**Square-based pyramid**	**Octahedron**	**Hemisphere**	**Sphere**
Four faces Four vertices Six edges	Five faces Five vertices Eight edges	Eight faces Six vertices Twelve edges	 One flat face and one curved face No vertices One curved edge	One curved face No vertices No edges

Area Formulae

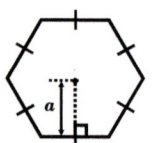
Area of a regular polygon = $\frac{1}{2}$ × apothem × perimeter
= $\frac{1}{2} \times a \times p$

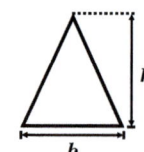
Area of a triangle = $\frac{1}{2}$ × base × perpendicular height
= $\frac{1}{2} \times b \times h$

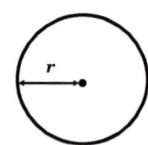
Area of a circle = pi × radius^2
= $\pi \times r^2$

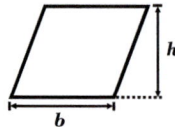
Area of a parallelogram = base × perpendicular height
= $b \times h$

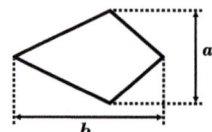
Area of a kite = $\frac{1}{2}$ × product of the two diagonals
= $\frac{1}{2} \times a \times b$

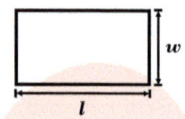
Area of a quadrilateral = length × width
= $l \times w$

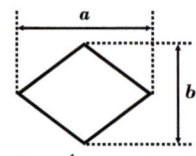
Area of a rhombus = $\frac{1}{2}$ × product of the two diagonals
= $\frac{1}{2} \times a \times b$

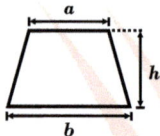
Area of a trapezium = $\frac{1}{2}$ × sum of the lengths of the parallel sides × perpendicular height
= $\frac{1}{2} \times (a + b) \times h$

Volume Formulae

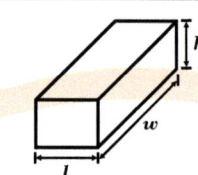
Volume of a cuboid = length × width × height
= $l \times w \times h$

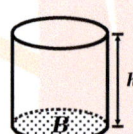
Volume of a prism = area of cross-section × height
= $B \times h$

Other Useful Formulae

Surface area of a 3D shape = sum of the areas of all the faces

Perimeter of a 2D shape = sum of the lengths of all the sides

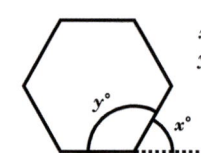
$x°$ is an exterior angle.
$y°$ is an interior angle.

An exterior angle of a regular polygon = $360°$ / number of sides
= $360°/n$

An interior angle of a regular polygon = $180°$ × (number of sides - 2) / number of sides
= $180° \times (n - 2)/n$

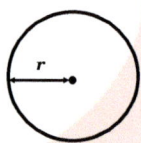
Circumference of a circle = 2 × pi × radius
= $2 \times \pi \times r$

Probability

A measure of how likely it is that a particular event will occur.
The probability of event A happening, P(A), is given by: number of ways in which event A can happen ÷ total number of possible outcomes.

'And' rule
The 'and' rule is used to find the probability of a combination of events occurring.

The probability of events A **and** B happening is:
$$P(A \text{ and } B) = P(A) \times P(B)$$

The word 'and' is replaced by a multiplication sign.

'Or' rule
The 'or' rule is used to find the probability of one or other event occurring.

The probability of event A **or** B happening is:
$$P(A \text{ or } B) = P(A) + P(B)$$

The word 'or' is replaced by an addition sign.

Tree diagram
One way of illustrating the probabilities of different events occurring is by using branches on a tree diagram. Each branch represents one possible event and is labelled with its probability.
e.g. a tree diagram illustrating two tosses of an unbiased coin

You can use the 'and' rule and the 'or' rule with the tree diagram: multiply probabilities along the branches, and add probabilities down the columns.

Probability scale
A scale that ranges from zero to one and measures the likelihood of an event occurring.

impossible — improbable — equally likely — probable — certain
0 — 0.25 — 0.5 — 0.75 — 1

- Picking out a black marble from a bag which contains only blue marbles
- A fair coin landing on heads
- Picking out a red marble from a bag which contains only red marbles

Remember that probabilities can be expressed as fractions, decimals or percentages.

Venn Diagrams

A diagram showing all logical relations for a collection of sets using overlapping ovals, non-overlapping ovals and a rectangular boundary.

e.g. a Venn diagram showing the first ten positive integers

The oval represents a set. A set is a collection of numbers that share a particular property. In this case, it is a set of triangular numbers.

The rectangle represents the universal set. The universal set contains all the elements in the sets within it. In this case, it is the set of the first ten positive integers.

Some useful Venn diagram patterns:

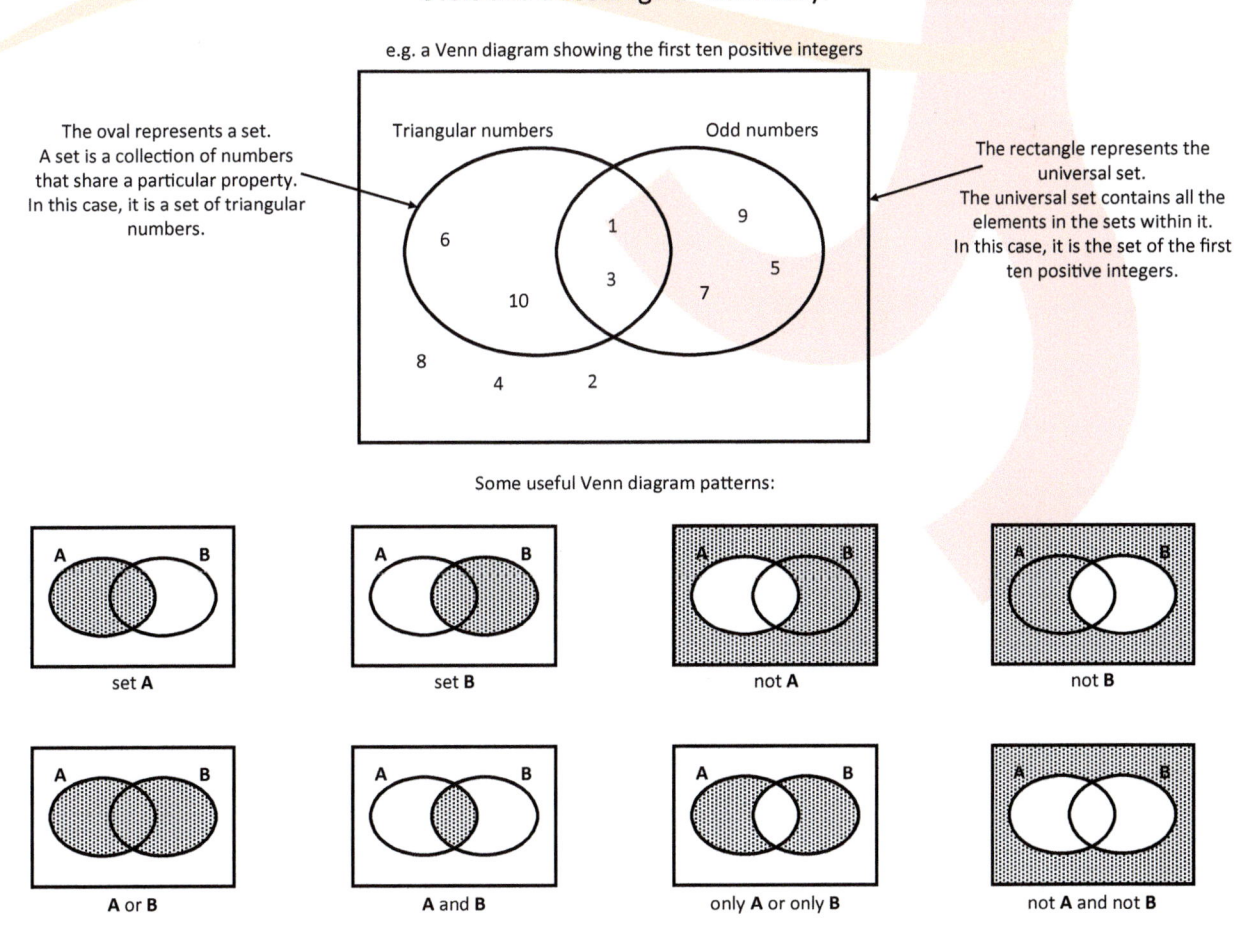

set **A** | set **B** | not **A** | not **B**

A or **B** | **A** and **B** | only **A** or only **B** | not **A** and not **B**

BLANK PAGE

MATHEMATICS

Multiple-Choice

Test A

Read the following instructions carefully:

1) Do not open this test paper until you are told to do so.

2) Please fill in your details accurately at the top of the answer sheet.

3) Only mark your answer using a **pencil** by drawing a **firm horizontal line** next to your chosen answer on the answer sheet.

4) If you want to change your answer, first rub out your old answer completely and then mark your new answer clearly.

5) Rulers, protractors or calculators are not allowed.

6) If you are unsure of the answer, choose the option you think is the best.

7) When you have finished a page, go straight onto the next page.

8) When you reach the end, go back and check all your answers.

9) Work as efficiently and carefully as you can to ensure you finish within time.

10) There are **50 questions** and you have **50 minutes** in which to complete this paper.

Good luck!

Copyright © ElevenPlusExams.co.uk 2019

All rights reserved. No part of this publication may be reproduced, stored or introduced into a retrieval system or transmitted in any form or by any means, without the prior written permission of the publisher nor may be circulated in any form of binding or cover other than the one in which it was published and without a similar condition including this condition being imposed on the subsequent publisher.

1

What is the size of angle $d°$ below?

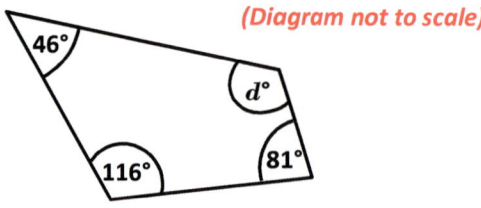
(Diagram not to scale)

2

What is the product of 17 and 101?

3

A structure consisting of two identical cuboids and a cylindrical section is shown below. The area of the circular base of the cylindrical section is 3m².

(Diagram not to scale)

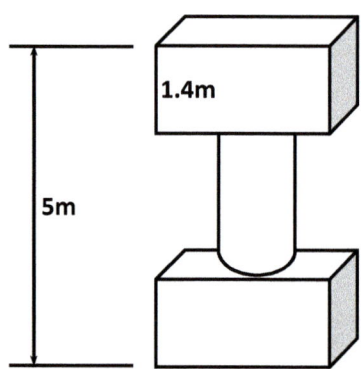

What is the volume of the cylindrical section?

4

What is $\sqrt{4} + 4^0 + 4^2 + 4^3$?

5

A circle and its diameter are shown below.

(Diagram not to scale)

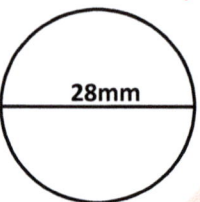

What is the radius of the circle in centimetres?

6

The chart shows the approximate conversion between ounces (oz) and grams (g).

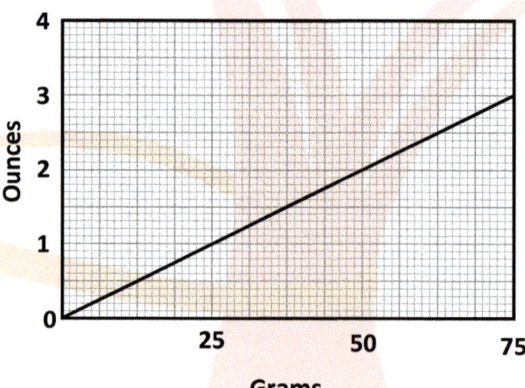

How many grams is 2.5 ounces?

7

What percentage of the capital letters in the grid below have rotational symmetry?

	A	I	
W	X	G	V
Q	O	T	P
Z	Y	C	R
	J	L	

A 25%   B 100%   C 50%   D 75%   E 0%

8

Gemma completed the following tasks one after another in the order they are shown without taking breaks. She started task 1 at 8am.

Task	Duration
1	50 minutes
2	25 minutes
3	1 hour
4	30 minutes
5	20 minutes
6	2 hours

How many tasks had she fully completed by half past eleven in the morning?

9

What is the perimeter of the symmetrical trapezium below?

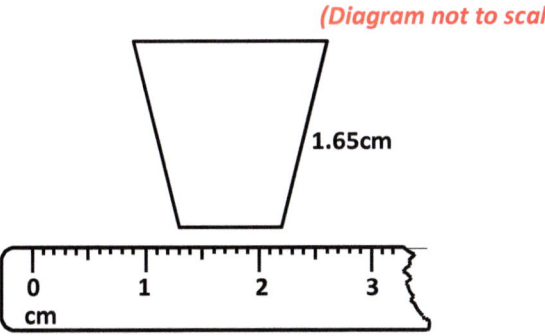

(Diagram not to scale)

10

What is the missing term in the number sequence below?

-91   -54   -17   ?   57   94

A 17   **B** -10   **C** 37   **D** -34   **E** 20

11

A colour is selected at random from red, orange, pink, yellow, green, purple, blue, grey and magenta. What is the probability that the colour selected has less than six letters in its name? Give your answer as a fraction.

12

What is the sixth multiple of twenty-nine?

13

What is the mode of the following numbers?

102   7   3   0   100   4   8   3   7   15   0   3

14

What are the coordinates of the lettered point which is directly east of point A?

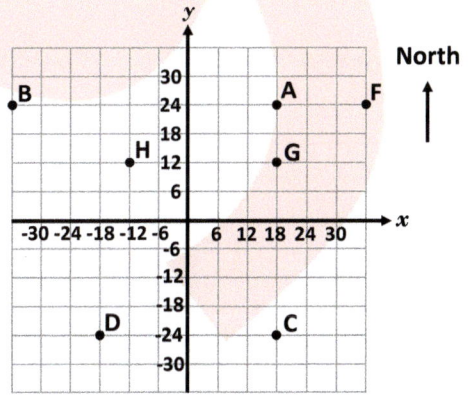

15

How many vertices does a square-based pyramid have?

PLEASE GO ON TO THE NEXT PAGE

16

How many 15ml spoons full of water would it take to fill the container below from empty to the level shown?

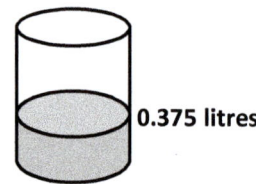
0.375 litres

17

A diamond is shown below on a grid of triangles.

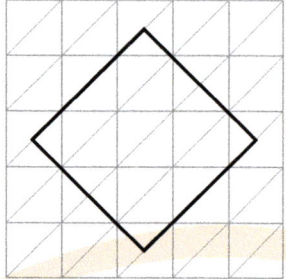

If each triangle that makes up the grid has an area of 2cm², what is the area of the diamond?

18

What is 75% of 96?

19

What is the total cost of four tomatoes, three carrots, three aubergines and two cucumbers?

Item	Cost per item
Aubergine	70p
Carrot	9p
Cucumber	70p
Tomato	18p

20

The hexagon below is rotated 90° clockwise about point Q.

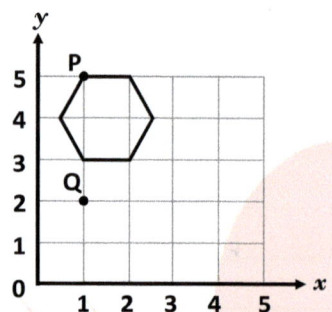

What are the new coordinates of point P?

21

What is the simplified expression for the perimeter of the shape below?

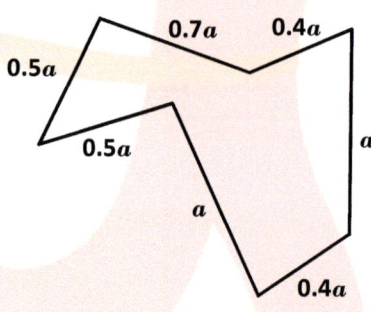

A $4.1a$ B $3.6a$ C $4.5a$ D $4.3a$ E $4a$

22

Express the sum of the shaded areas below as a mixed number.

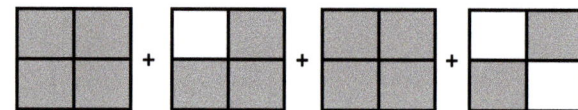

23

Martina selects the polygons from the shapes below. She then calculates the percentage of the polygons that are quadrilaterals.

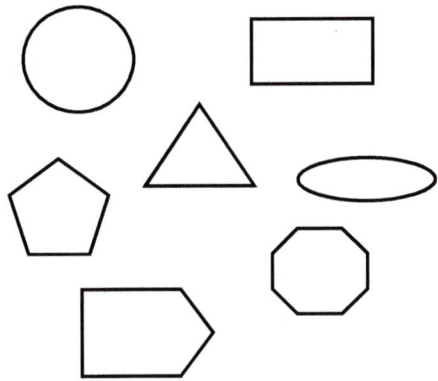

What is the correct answer?

24

What is the input to the number machine below?

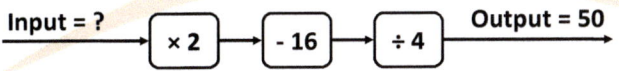

25

What is five hundred and sixteen minus a quarter of one hundred?

26

Which bar (labelled A to E) on the chart below shows the value of 27 rounded to the nearest 10?

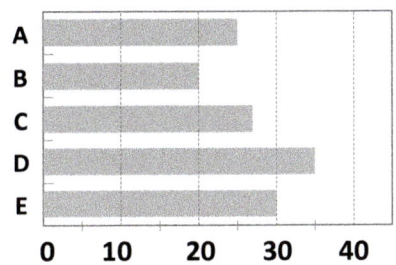

27

What is 0.96 ÷ 0.03?

28

On a road the ratio of cars to buses is 53:2. There are six buses. How many cars are there?

29

What is the missing term in the number sequence below?

?   24   6 $1\frac{1}{2}$ $\frac{3}{8}$

30

How many of the angles below are either acute or obtuse?

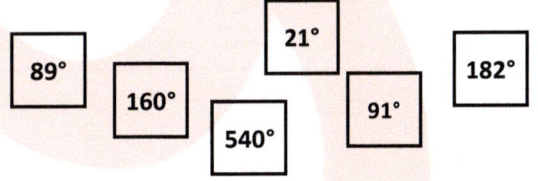

31

Kevin writes the fraction $\frac{60}{126}$ in its lowest terms. What is the denominator of the simplified fraction?

A 30   **B** 21   **C** 63   **D** 10   **E** 42

32

Daily temperatures are shown on the chart below.

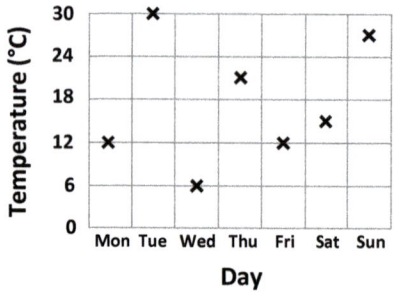

On how many days was the temperature no more than 12°C?

33

What temperature is shown on the thermometer?

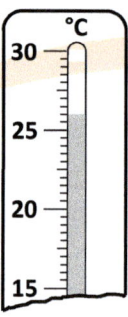

34

Renu bought an item for £2.61 with a £5 note.

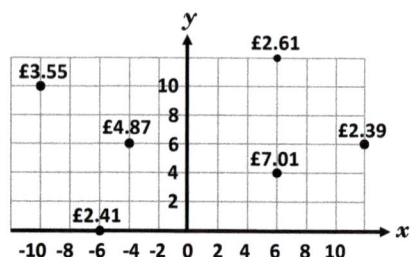

What are the coordinates which show the amount of change she received?

35

What is the area of the shape below?

(Diagram not to scale)

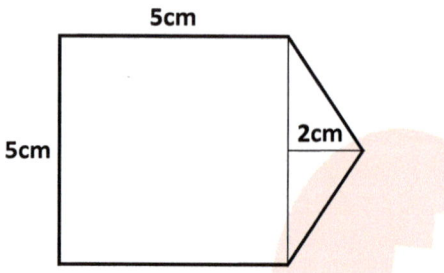

36

The net of a 3D shape is shown below.

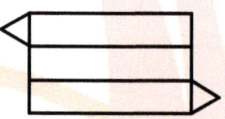

Which option (labelled A to E) is the name for the shape that is formed when the net is folded up?

A pentagonal prism
B triangular-based pyramid
C square-based pyramid
D triangular prism
E cone

37

What is the value of the question mark in the addition problem below?

| 12 | + | 15 | + | ? | = | 64 |

38

A small boat is shown below.

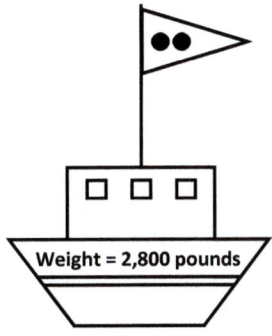

Approximately, what is the weight of the boat in kilograms (kg)?
Hint: 14 pounds (lb) ≈ 6 kilograms (kg).

39

A function machine multiplies its input by 8 and adds 60 to the result to get the output. The input is 19. What is the output number?

40

A page from a planner is shown below.

Mon 14th December	Thu 17th December	
Tue 15th December	Fri 18th December	
Wed 16th December	Sat 19th Dec	Sun 20th Dec

What day of the week was third of December?

41

What is the range of the numbers on the counters below?

42

Ruth bought 20 identical pens. She paid £30 for the pens and received £6 in change. How much did each pen cost?

43

What is the value of 9.1945 to the nearest hundredth?

44

What is the volume of the cuboid below?

(Diagram not to scale)

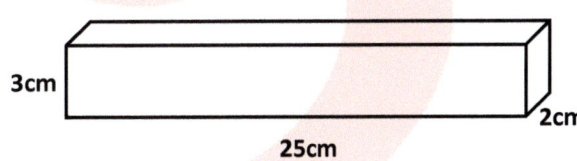

45

If $240 ÷ 15 = 4x$, what is the value of x?

A 5   B 16   C 64   D 8   E 4

46

Part of a shape is shown below along with a line of symmetry.

How many corners are on the full shape?

47

What is the fifth prime number?

48

The Town Hall on the grid below is translated down three squares and left four squares.

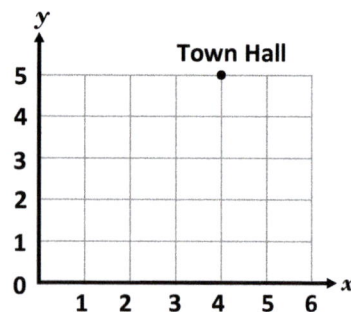

What are the new coordinates of the Town Hall?

49

What is $(2{,}450 \div 12.5) \times 0$?

A 1
B 196
C 0
D 99
E 197

50

A square on the grid below is selected at random.

What is the probability that the square is empty?

A $\frac{12}{39}$
B $\frac{23}{35}$
C $\frac{2}{3}$
D $\frac{21}{32}$
E $\frac{12}{34}$

END OF TEST

MATHEMATICS

Multiple-Choice

Test B

Read the following instructions carefully:

1) Do not open this test paper until you are told to do so.

2) Please fill in your details accurately at the top of the answer sheet.

3) Only mark your answer using a **pencil** by drawing a **firm horizontal line** next to your chosen answer on the answer sheet.

4) If you want to change your answer, first rub out your old answer completely and then mark your new answer clearly.

5) Rulers, protractors or calculators are not allowed.

6) If you are unsure of the answer, choose the option you think is the best.

7) When you have finished a page, go straight onto the next page.

8) When you reach the end, go back and check all your answers.

9) Work as efficiently and carefully as you can to ensure you finish within time.

10) There are **50 questions** and you have **50 minutes** in which to complete this paper.

Good luck!

Copyright © ElevenPlusExams.co.uk 2019

All rights reserved. No part of this publication may be reproduced, stored or introduced into a retrieval system or transmitted in any form or by any means, without the prior written permission of the publisher nor may be circulated in any form of binding or cover other than the one in which it was published and without a similar condition including this condition being imposed on the subsequent publisher.

1

A map is produced to a scale of 1:270. What distance in metres would be represented by 40mm on the map?

2

Which answer (labelled A to E) below represents respectively the lettered points at coordinates (-60, 30), (20, 10), (-60, -30) and (40, -30)?

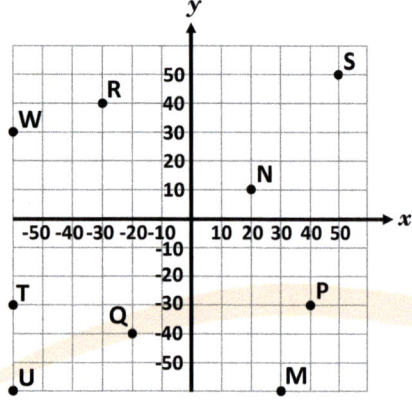

- **A** MNWR
- **B** WNTP
- **C** WNTR
- **D** MNTP
- **E** UPRW

3

Increase 625 by 34.

4

What is $^7/_3 \times 18$?

5

300 people were asked which colour pen they mainly use. The results are shown in the pie chart below.

(Diagram not to scale)

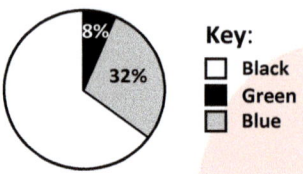

Key:
- ☐ Black
- ■ Green
- ▨ Blue

How many people mainly used black pens?

6

The volume of the whole shape below is 120cm^3.

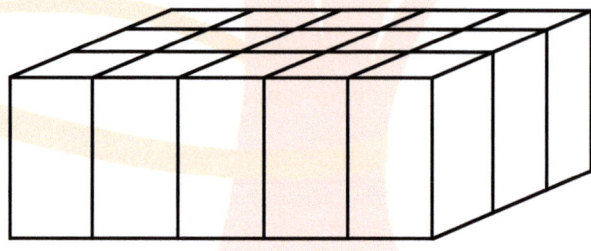

What is the volume of one of the identical cuboids which make up the whole shape?

7

How many faces does the shape below have?

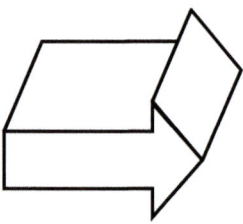

A 9   **B** 8   **C** 3   **D** 7   **E** 5

PLEASE GO ON TO THE NEXT PAGE

8

The clock face below shows the time one afternoon.

What time in 12-hour clock format is a quarter of an hour after the time shown on the clock face?

A 3.15pm   B 14:55   C 2.45pm   D 3.25pm   E 15:20

9

Summary data for the waist sizes of a group of people are shown in the table below.

Waist size (inches)	26	28	30	32	34
Frequency	3	8	3	2	3

What is the median waist size of the group?

10

Some letters are shown inside the oblong below.

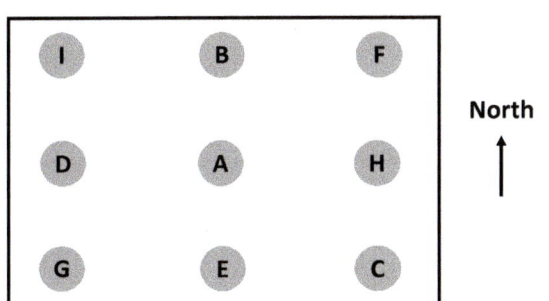

Which letter is both directly south of B and directly east of G?

11

Guy bought some shopping totalling £10.97 with a ten pound note, a fifty pence coin and three twenty pence coins. How much change would Guy have received?

12

What is the output of the Roman numeral number machine below? Give the output in Roman numerals.

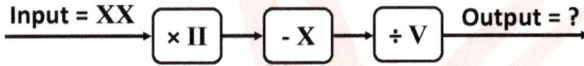

13

What is the next term in the number sequence below?

0   2   2   4   4   8   6   16   ?

14

How many of the bars on the chart below represent values which are factors of 42?

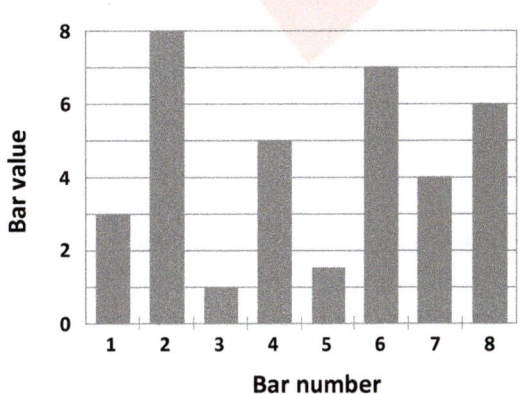

15

What is 210 ÷ 8?

16

How many lines of symmetry does the regular polygon below have?

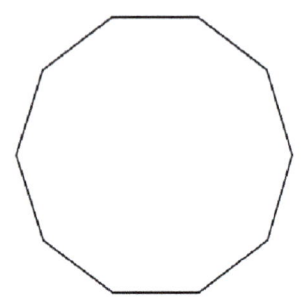

17

How many sides on the shape below are perpendicular to side A?

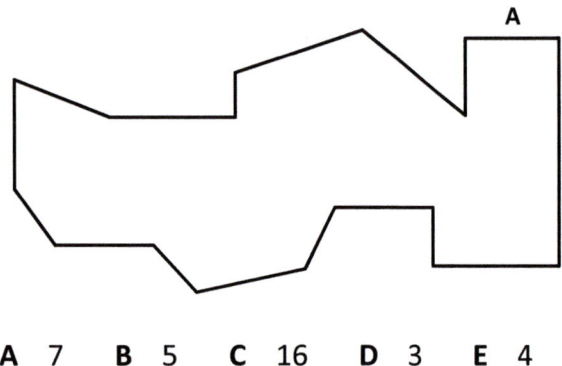

A 7 **B** 5 **C** 16 **D** 3 **E** 4

18

Two fair dice are rolled. What is the probability that the first will show a value of more than two and the second will show a value of at least four?

19

The cylinder below is rotated 270° clockwise. Which answer (lettered A to E) shows its new position?

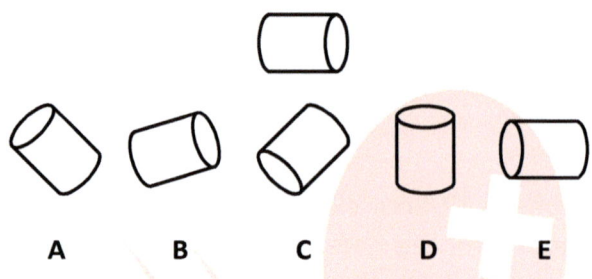

20

What is the height of the bus below in millimetres?

(Diagram not to scale)

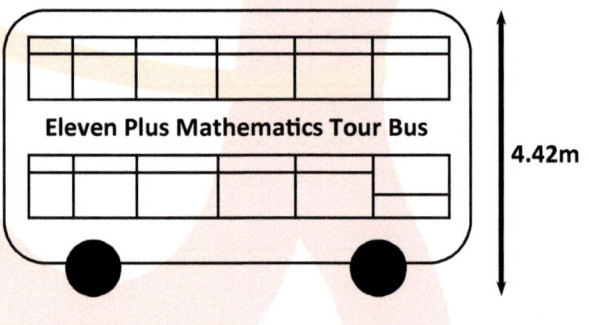

21

What is the area of the square below?

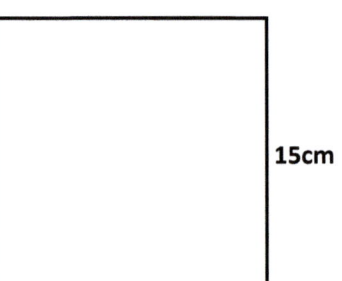

PLEASE GO ON TO THE NEXT PAGE

22

The shapes below are all worth a number of points. Each trapezium is worth four points, each parallelogram is worth five points and each triangle is worth two points. The number of points for each hexagon is identical and is unknown. The total number of points for all eight shapes is 39.

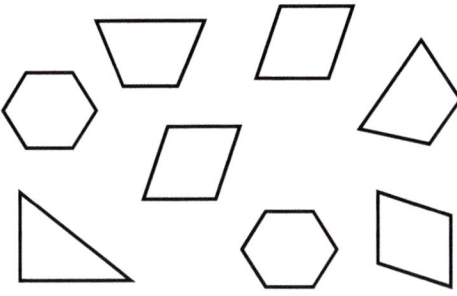

How many points is each hexagon worth?

___

23

What is the value of the underlined digit in 28̲1,902?

___

24

The test scores for four students are shown below.

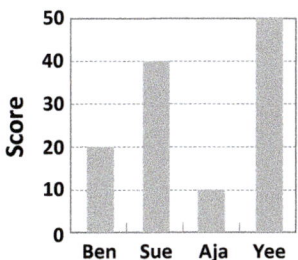

What percentage of students scored less than 10?

25

What is the difference between 27.58 and 22.9?

___

26

The cuboids shown below are a repeating pattern. How many cuboids are there altogether if there are twelve unshaded cuboids?

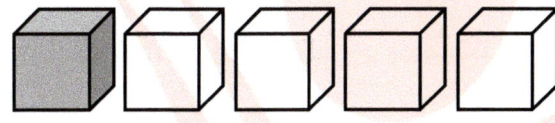

___

27

What is the sum of the third cube number and the third triangular number?

___

28

The front of a shed is shown below. The area of the triangular top section is $1m^2$. The area of each of the two door panels is $0.65m^2$. The whole area of the front of the shed is $5m^2$.

(Diagram not to scale)

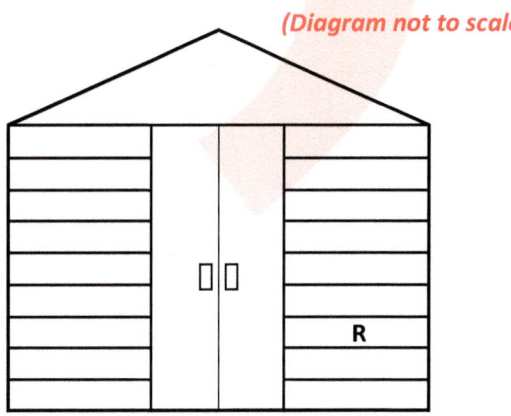

What is the area of one of the identical panels (labelled R) on the front of the shed?

PLEASE GO ON TO THE NEXT PAGE

29

Point H at coordinates (5, 5) is rotated 90° clockwise about the point (0, 0). What are the new coordinates of point H?

30

What is the input to the number machine below?

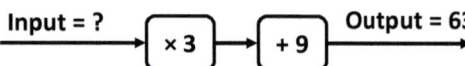

31

What is the lowest common multiple (LCM) of 6 and 14?

A 28   **B** 42   **C** 24   **D** 84   **E** 30

32

What is the combined amount of liquid in the jugs below?

(Diagrams not to scale)

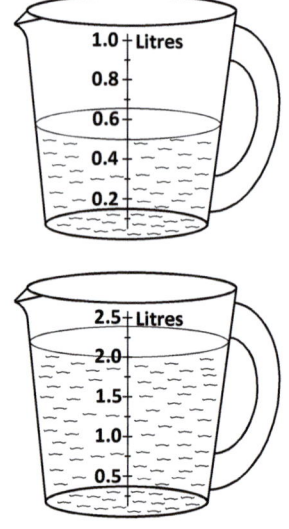

33

What is the size of angle $x°$ below?

(Diagram not to scale)

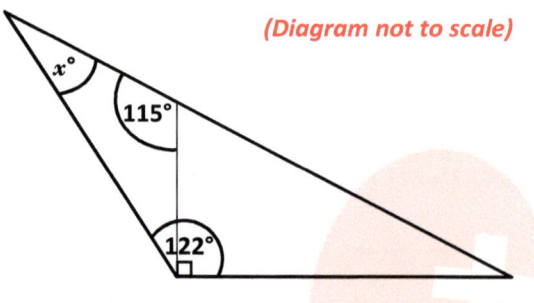

34

What is the volume of the cuboid below?

(Diagram not to scale)

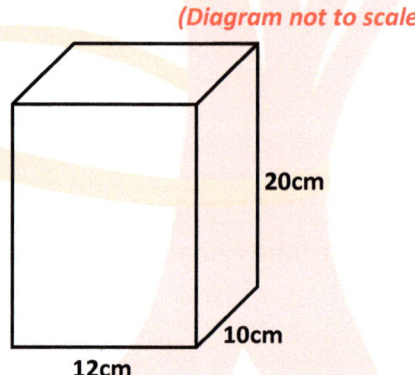

35

What are the coordinates of point Z?

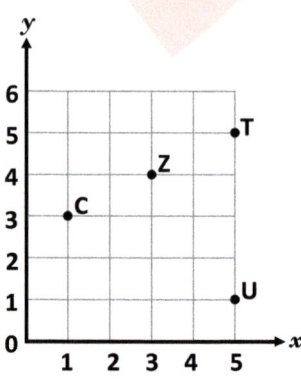

36

Expressed in its lowest terms, what fraction of the shape below is shaded?

37

The table below shows the number of books available in a shop.

No. of books available	No. of pages	Fiction or non fiction?	Have pictures?
3	50	Fiction	No
6	75	Fiction	Yes
8	100	Non fiction	No
4	125	Fiction	Yes
1	150	Non fiction	No

How many books have more than 90 pages and do not have any pictures?

38

A net of a 3D shape is shown below.

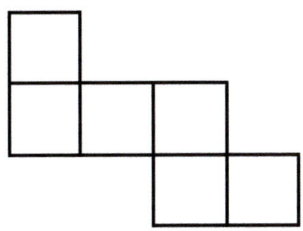

How many edges will the 3D shape have once the net is folded up?

39

Reduce 174 by 48.

40

An alarm clock is shown below. The alarm is set to sound at 14:10. The current time is shown on the screen.

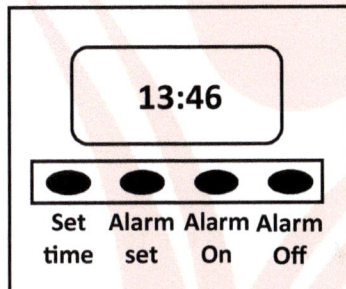

In how many minutes will the alarm sound?

41

If it rained on 18 days during November, on what percentage of days in the month did it rain on?

A 60%   B 80%   C 50%   D 40%   E 66.7%

42

A shape is selected at random from those shown below.

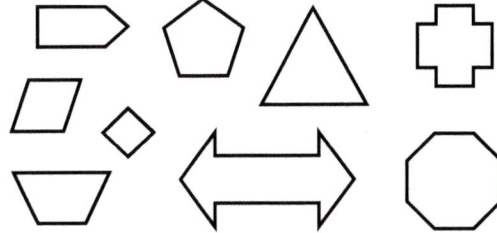

What is the probability it has less than six sides?

43

What is the result of rounding 39.09 to the nearest whole number?

44

What is 1 × 2 × 3 × 5?

45

The chart below shows the temperatures over seven days.

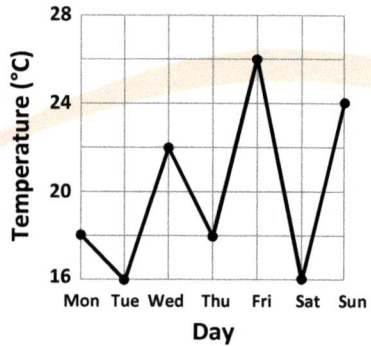

What is the average daily temperature over all seven days?

46

The radius of the circle below is 6cm.

(Diagram not to scale)

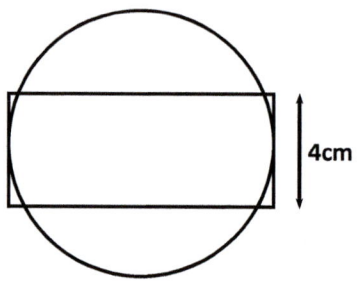

What is the perimeter of the rectangle?

47

If $7a = 35$, what is the value of a?

48

An arrow is shown below along with two lines of symmetry. Which answer (labelled A to E) shows the direction of the arrow in quadrant Q?

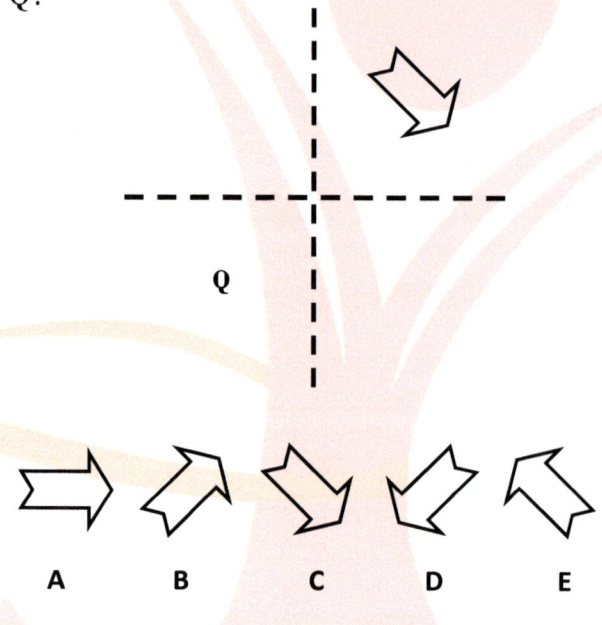

49

A car weighs 1.983 tonnes. What is its weight in kilograms?

50

What year is given by Roman numerals MMXX?

END OF TEST

MATHEMATICS

Multiple-Choice

Test C

Read the following instructions carefully:

1) Do not open this test paper until you are told to do so.

2) Please fill in your details accurately at the top of the answer sheet.

3) Only mark your answer using a **pencil** by drawing a **firm horizontal line** next to your chosen answer on the answer sheet.

4) If you want to change your answer, first rub out your old answer completely and then mark your new answer clearly.

5) Rulers, protractors or calculators are not allowed.

6) If you are unsure of the answer, choose the option you think is the best.

7) When you have finished a page, go straight onto the next page.

8) When you reach the end, go back and check all your answers.

9) Work as efficiently and carefully as you can to ensure you finish within time.

10) There are **50 questions** and you have **50 minutes** in which to complete this paper.

Good luck!

Copyright © ElevenPlusExams.co.uk 2019

All rights reserved. No part of this publication may be reproduced, stored or introduced into a retrieval system or transmitted in any form or by any means, without the prior written permission of the publisher nor may be circulated in any form of binding or cover other than the one in which it was published and without a similar condition including this condition being imposed on the subsequent publisher.

1

What is seventy-two multiplied by three?

A 24   B 186   C 216   D 75   E 144

2

The brick wall below consists of a number of larger identical bricks and four identical smaller bricks. Each smaller brick is half the weight of a larger brick. Each larger brick is 3.5kg.

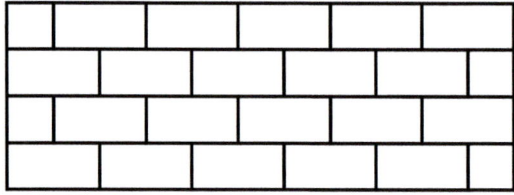

What is the total weight of the bricks in the wall?

3

What is the sum of the two missing values in the sequence below?

46   41   36   31   26   ?   ?

4

What are the coordinates of the lettered point directly below point K on the grid?

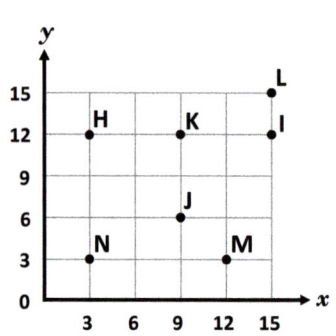

5

A regular hexagon and rectangle are shown below.

(Diagram not to scale)

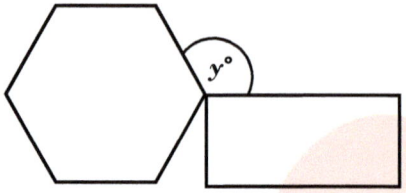

What is the size of angle $y°$?

6

A group of people were asked if they liked red (R) grapes and green (G) grapes. The results are shown in the Venn diagram below.

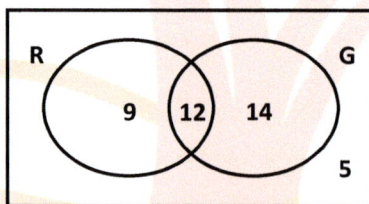

What percentage of people liked both red and green grapes?

7

The table below shows times for the next five trains departing Radley station.

Destination	Platform	Departure Time
Paddington	2	15:12
Oxford	2	15:16
Paddington	2	15:42
Oxford	1	15:51
Oxford	1	15:57

If the time now is 2.58pm, how many trains would depart from Radley station in the next three-quarters of an hour?

PLEASE GO ON TO THE NEXT PAGE

8

What is the volume of the shape below?

(Diagram not to scale)

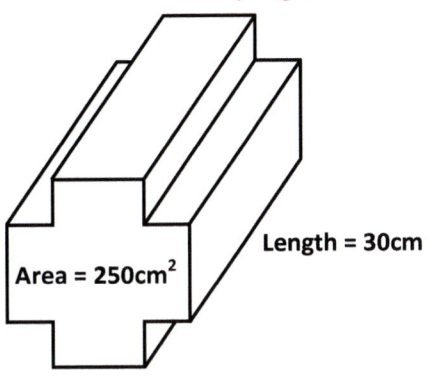

9

If 5(x - 4) = 10, what is the value of x?

A 4   **B** 6   **C** 2   **D** 10   **E** 5

10

Expressed in its lowest terms, what is the ratio of acute-angled triangles to obtuse-angled triangles below?

11

What is the difference between the number of edges in an octagonal prism and a tetrahedron?

12

The perimeter of the rectangle below is 30cm.

(Diagram not to scale)

What is the area of the rectangle?

13

The total cost of six identical comics is £16.50. How much does each comic cost?

14

What is the average of the two readings on the scales below?

(Diagrams not to scale)

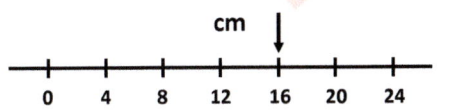

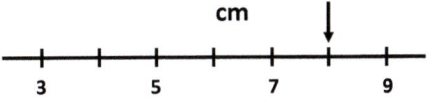

15

Pietro is collecting cards. He has 187 unique cards and needs 49 more to complete his collection. How many cards in total are in the entire collection?

16

What is the order of rotational symmetry for the shape below?

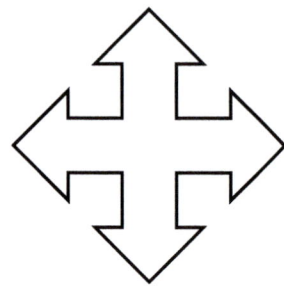

17

What is the sum of all the numbers between 40 and 70, that are exactly divisible by 13?

18

The parallelogram is reflected in the x-axis. The kite is translated down 14 units and right 16 units.

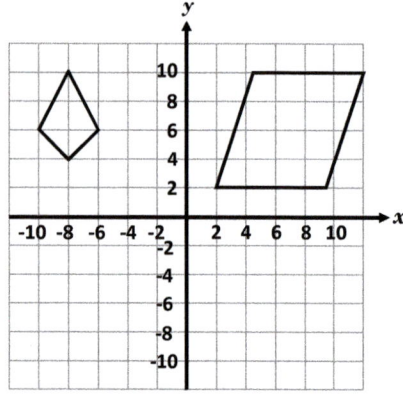

At which coordinates does a corner of the kite touch a side of the reflected parallelogram?

19

A dataset consists of three numbers. One number occurs twice and the other occurs once. The chart below shows the mode, mean, median and range of the dataset.

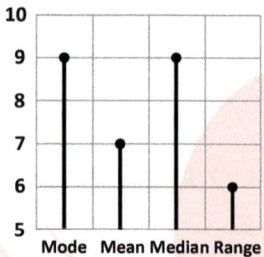

What is the smallest number in the dataset?

20

What percentage of values in the shapes below are square numbers?

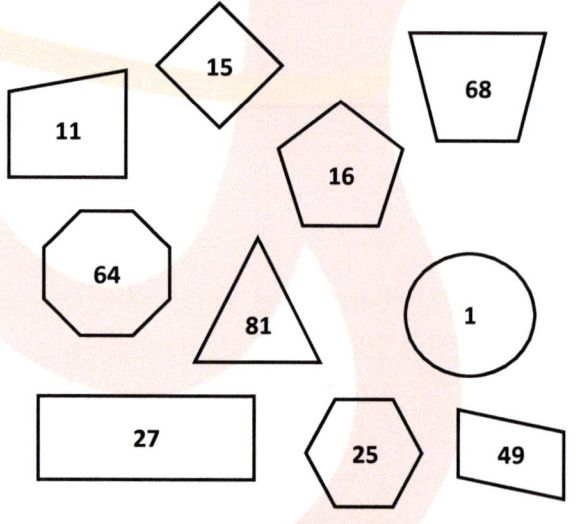

21

What is $3/5 - 1/2$?

A $11/10$ **B** $1/3$ **C** $1/10$ **D** $2/3$ **E** $1/5$

PLEASE GO ON TO THE NEXT PAGE

22

Which of the following (labelled A to E) is not a term relating to part of a circle?

A Circumference
B Arc
C Radius
D Diameter
E Vertex

23

A disc is selected at random from those below.

What is the probability that the disc will have an odd number on it?

24

A steam train is shown below.

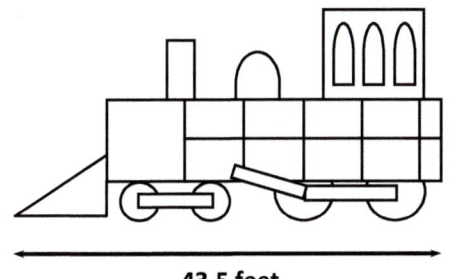

(Diagram not to scale)

43.5 feet

What is its length in yards?
Hint: 1 yard (yd) = 3 feet.

25

What is 4.7965 correct to two decimal places?

26

Big Ben below shows the time one evening. What time is shown? Give your answer in 24-hour clock format.

27

What is the positive square root of one hundred and forty-four?

A 10   B 12   C 16   D 14   E 13

28

What is the output of the number machine below?

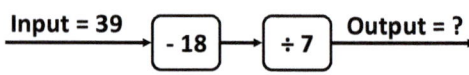

A 147   B 21   C 9   D 14   E 3

29

What is the difference in height between a zebra at 1.35m and a fox at 48cm?

30

Approximately, what is the weight in stones of the scale below?
Hint: 1 stone ≈ 6kg.

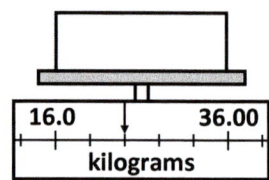

31

What is the largest prime factor of 68?

A 17
B 68
C 2
D 4
E 34

32

What is the perimeter of the shape below?

(Diagram not to scale)

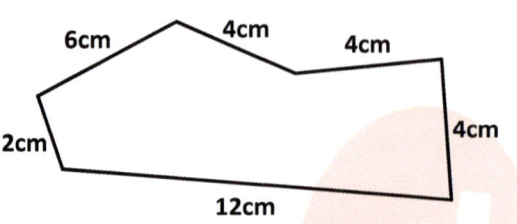

33

In what direction is the factory from the car park?

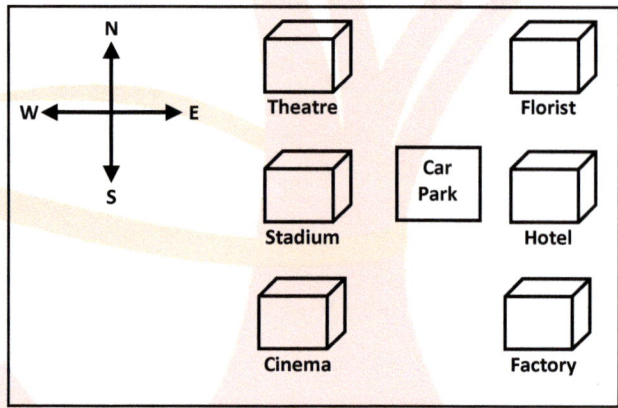

34

Which answer (labelled A to E) is the name of the shape shown below?

A Triangular prism
B Tetrahedron
C Cylinder
D Cone
E Triangular-based pyramid

PLEASE GO ON TO THE NEXT PAGE

35

What is the volume of the cube below?

(Diagram not to scale)

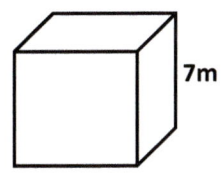

36

What is the probability that the spinner lands on a number less than 30 when spun?

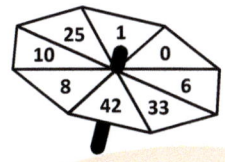

37

Part of a shape is shown below along with two lines of symmetry.

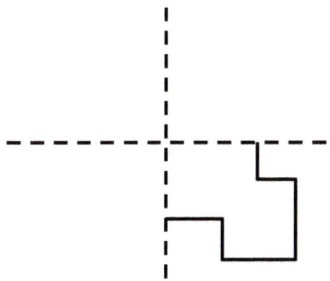

How many corners are on the full shape?

A 10   **B** 28   **C** 20   **D** 14   **E** 15

38

The line chart below shows the distance travelled over time by a car.

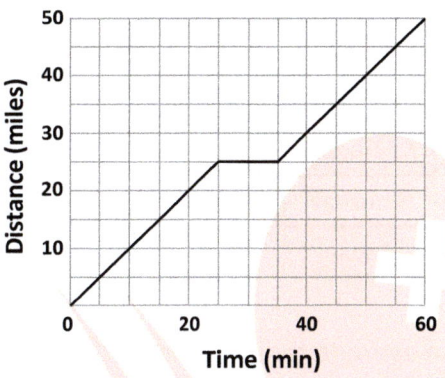

How many miles had the car travelled after 55 minutes?

39

What are the midpoint coordinates of the line AB on the grid below?

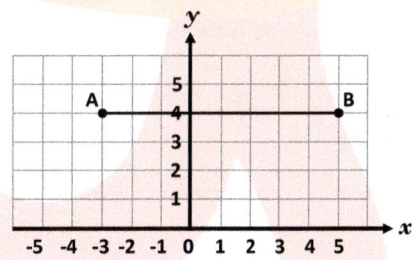

40

In a shop, DVDs usually sell for £10 each and CDs sell for £8 each. During a sale, the price of each DVD is reduced by 20% and the price of each CD is reduced by 25%. Tala buys four DVDs and three CDs in the sale period. How much does she pay in total for the items?

PLEASE GO ON TO THE NEXT PAGE

41

Five temperatures are shown below.

Day	Temp (°C)
Monday	9
Tuesday	2
Wednesday	12
Thursday	14
Friday	8

What is the average temperature?

42

How many below 12 is -25?

43

What is the missing number in the sequence below?

    0.8   0.4   0.2   0.1   ?

44

What is the input to the number machine below?

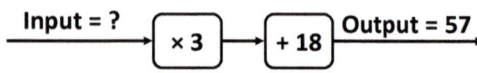

A 25   **B** 13   **C** 18   **D** 57   **E** 225

45

What is $\frac{3}{7} \div 3$?

46

Approximately, how many gallons of water are in the watering can below?
Hint: 1 gallon (gal) ≈ 4 litres (l).

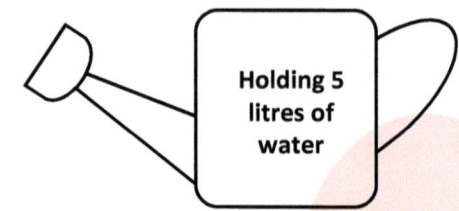

47

A box contains 5p and 10p coins in the ratio 3:5. There are twelve 5p coins in the box. How much money in total does the box contain?

48

Phillip has 139 shapes identical to the shape below. How many sides are there in total on all 139 shapes?

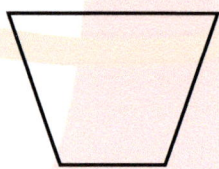

49

If £38 is split equally between four people, how much money does each person receive?

50

What is the expression for the perimeter of the parallelogram below?

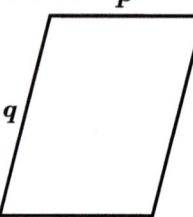

END OF TEST

MATHEMATICS

Multiple-Choice

Test D

Read the following instructions carefully:

1) Do not open this test paper until you are told to do so.

2) Please fill in your details accurately at the top of the answer sheet.

3) Only mark your answer using a **pencil** by drawing a **firm horizontal line** next to your chosen answer on the answer sheet.

4) If you want to change your answer, first rub out your old answer completely and then mark your new answer clearly.

5) Rulers, protractors or calculators are not allowed.

6) If you are unsure of the answer, choose the option you think is the best.

7) When you have finished a page, go straight onto the next page.

8) When you reach the end, go back and check all your answers.

9) Work as efficiently and carefully as you can to ensure you finish within time.

10) There are **50 questions** and you have **50 minutes** in which to complete this paper.

Good luck!

Copyright © ElevenPlusExams.co.uk 2019

All rights reserved. No part of this publication may be reproduced, stored or introduced into a retrieval system or transmitted in any form or by any means, without the prior written permission of the publisher nor may be circulated in any form of binding or cover other than the one in which it was published and without a similar condition including this condition being imposed on the subsequent publisher.

1

What is the lowest common multiple (LCM) of 4, 5 and 8?

_____

2

Triangle T is translated two squares down and five squares right.

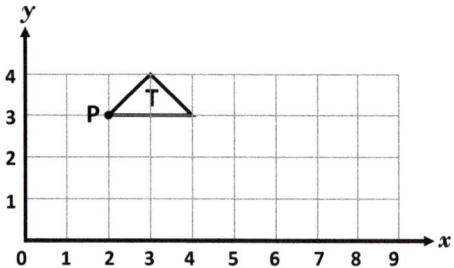

What are the new coordinates of point *P*?

_____

3

What is the difference between 36.28 and 19.57?

_____

4

How many of the five 3D shapes below have a prime or cubic number of faces?

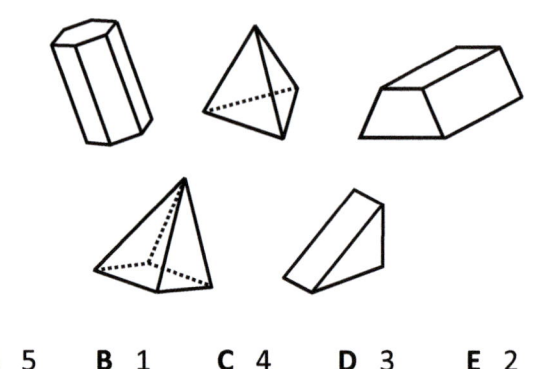

A 5   B 1   C 4   D 3   E 2

5

What is the sum of the two numbers missing in the sequence below?

2 ? 5 7 11 13 ? 19 23

_____

6

The table shows the number of mobile phones sold by a department store over a five week period.

	Week 1	Week 2	Week 3	Week 4	Week 5
Mon	13	12	18	16	22
Tue	10	14	19	18	20
Wed	11	15	16	19	24
Thu	14	12	17	18	22
Fri	15	11	20	16	19

The number of phones sold for one of the five weeks is plotted below.

(Diagram not to scale)

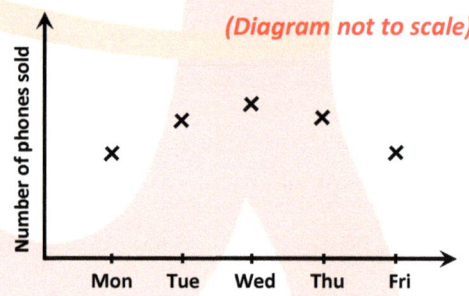

Which week is it?

_____

7

The 2,220m long Humber Bridge was first opened to traffic in June 1981.

A drawing of the bridge is to be created on paper using a scale of 1:10,000.

How long will the bridge be on the drawing in centimetres?

PLEASE GO ON TO THE NEXT PAGE

8

Children in a Year six class were asked their favourite colour. The results are shown in the Venn diagram below.

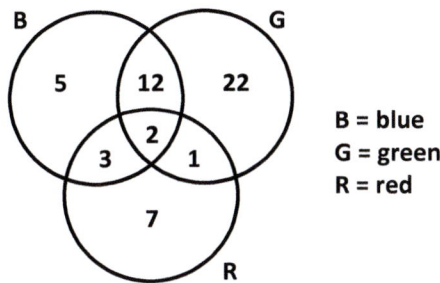

B = blue
G = green
R = red

How many children like both blue and green but not red?

A 2   B 45   C 27   D 39   E 12

9

What fraction, when divided by $^1/_3$, results in an answer of $^3/_2$?

10

Look at the simplified restaurant menu below.

All starters.........................£2.50
All main courses...............£6.00
All desserts........................£3.00
10% service charge added to all bills

Kushal orders a starter, a main course and a dessert.

How much does Kushal pay in total for the order?

11

A function machine subtracts 3 from the input number and multiplies the result by 7. Finally, 18 is added to give an output of 53.

What was the input number?

12

TV 1 is priced at £A and TV 2 is 1.3 times the price of TV 1.

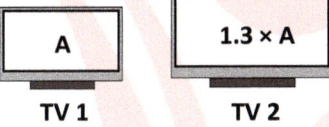

TV 1   TV 2

If TV 1 is priced at £275, what is the cost of TV 2?

13

Express the time twenty-six minutes after three in the morning in 24-hour clock notation?

14

The table below shows distances travelled by Jane over a five day period. The two missing distances are the same.

Day	Distance (km)
Mon	10
Tue	?
Wed	5
Thu	?
Fri	7

If the mean distance was 6km, how many km did Jane travel on Thursday?

PLEASE GO ON TO THE NEXT PAGE

15

What is 29.08 rounded to the nearest tenth?

16

Leon gives a percentage of his 40 counters to each of his friends as shown in the pie chart below.

(Diagram not to scale)

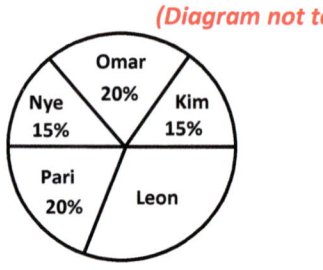

How many counters did Leon keep for himself?

17

Kamal cut 80cm off a 2.5m length of plastic tubing.

What percentage of the tubing was left?

18

Look at the five identical shelves below.

(Diagram not to scale)

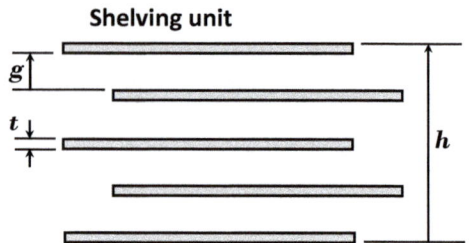

The total height (h) of the shelving unit is 1.1m and the gap (g) between adjacent shelves is 25cm.

What is the thickness (t) of each shelf in mm?

19

Eight test marks are given below.

3 4 3 5 5 6 4 5

What is the product of the mode and median scores?

20

The three different voltmeters shown below are used to measure the supply voltage at a particular house.

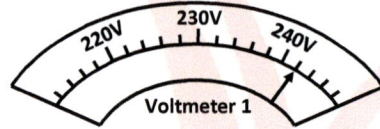

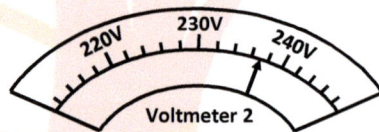

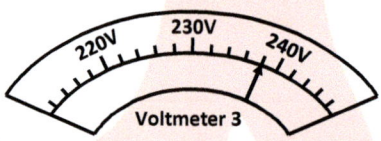

Use the three scale readings to work out the mean voltage in volts (V).

21

A newspaper advert has a standard cost of £30, plus 20p per word. For a total advert cost of £50, how many words would the advert have?

A 100   B 75   C 50   D 200   E 120

PLEASE GO ON TO THE NEXT PAGE

22

The diagram below comprises of an equilateral triangle T1, a symmetrical trapezium T2 and a right-angled triangle T3.

(Diagram not to scale)

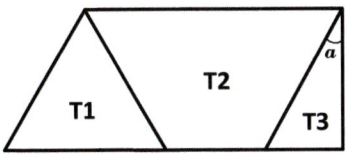

Determine the size of angle a.

23

The left end coordinates of a horizontal line are (3, 4).

Which one of the following coordinates could be another point on the same line?

(2, 4)   (5, 5)   (0, 4)   (6, 8)   (4, 4)

24

$$T = 24 + 19n$$

Which of these is a rearranged version of the equation above?

A $n = (24 - T)/19$
B $n = (T + 24)/19$
C $n = (T - 24)/19$
D $n = (T - 19)/24$
E $n = (19 + T)/24$

25

Prasha buys a bag of potatoes for £1.29 and six eggs for £1.70. She pays with a £5 note.

How much change does Prasha receive?

26

The fair die below is rolled and the coin is thrown.

What is the probability that the coin shows tails and the die shows a number greater than four?

27

The length of a rectangle is twice its width. If its length is 3m, what is the perimeter of the rectangle?

28

The angles in the triangle are in the ratio 1:2:6.

(Diagram not to scale)

What is the size of the largest angle expressed in degrees?

29

The rule for finding the nth term in a sequence is $5n$.

What is the sum of the fourth and seventh terms?

30

Each edge of Box 1 is 60cm long and each edge of Box 2 is 15cm long.

(Diagram not to scale)

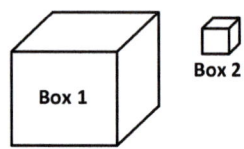

How many Box 2's can be packed into Box 1?

31

The prime factorisation process of a number N revealed prime factors of 2, 3, 3 and 5.

What was the number N?

32

Part of a whole shape along with two mirror lines M1 and M2 are shown below.

(Diagram not to scale)

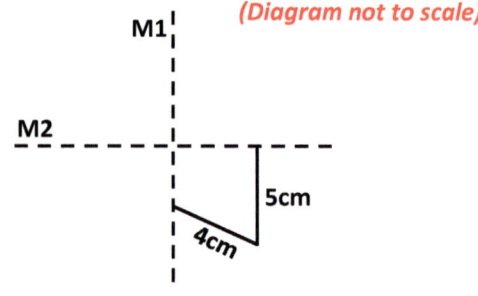

What is the distance around the outside of the whole shape?

33

A cuboid has a width of 5cm, a height of 4cm and a volume of 160cm^3.

What is its length in millimetres (mm)?

34

Points P, Q and R on the grid below are three corners of a parallelogram.

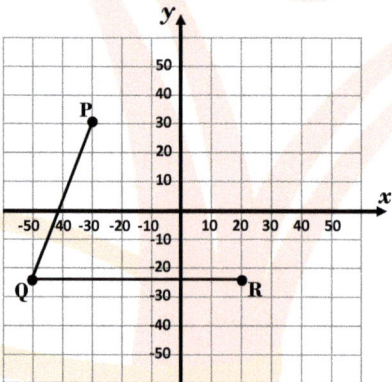

What are the coordinates of the fourth corner?

35

Work out the value of A in the number grid below.

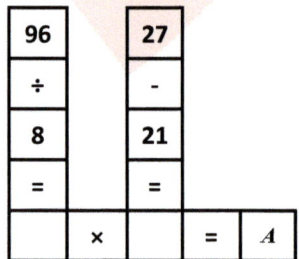

A 72   B 66   C 2   D 78   E 576

PLEASE GO ON TO THE NEXT PAGE

36

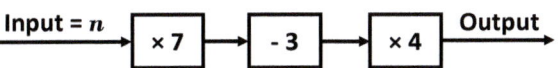

Which of the following expressions could be used to obtain the output of the number machine above?

7(3n + 4)
28n + 3
3(7n - 4)
28n - 12
12n - 21

37

The words below describe the chance of an event happening.

Impossible   Unlikely   Evens   Likely   Certain

Which one of the events below could be described as being likely?

A   A tossed coin will show tails seven times in a row.
B   The next child born at a local hospital will be a girl.
C   It will rain at least once in April.
D   There will be 31 days in February next year.
E   The sun will rise tomorrow.

38

A single straight line is drawn inside the shape below to split the regular pentagon into two different common 2D shapes.

Which option below lists the two possible shapes?

A   kite and parallelogram
B   triangle and trapezium
C   trapezium and rectangle
D   rectangle and kite
E   square and rhombus

39

Which one of these statements is untrue?

A   A reflex angle is between 90° and 180°.
B   Parallel lines never cross.
C   Interior angles of a square sum to 360°.
D   Oblique lines are neither horizontal nor vertical.
E   A bearing is the angle between North and the direction in which something is travelling.

40

The shape below shows an isosceles triangle CDE inside a rectangle ABCD.

(Diagram not to scale)

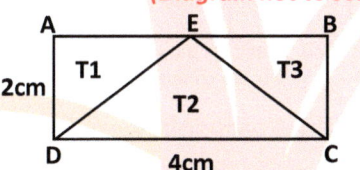

What is the combined area of triangles T1 and T2?

41

A 2D shape has the following properties:
* All four sides are of equal length.
* Opposite sides are parallel.
* Diagonally opposite angles are equal.
* The diagonals bisect each other at 90°.

What is the name of the 2D shape?

42

What is the sum of the fractions represented by the shaded areas of the shapes below?

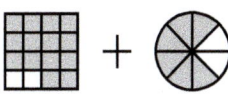

Express your final answer in mixed number format.

PLEASE GO ON TO THE NEXT PAGE

43

Given that 1 stone = 14lb and 1lb ≈ 450g.

Express the weight of a 0.5 stone parcel in kg.

44

The bar chart below shows the number of cars sold at a garage over a three month period.

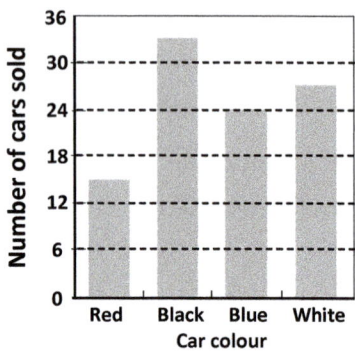

What fraction of the cars sold were black in colour?

45

There are 27 children in an after school group. If there are five boys to every four girls, how many boys are in the group?

46

$$t = 20 - 4s$$

The table below shows some values of s and t based on the formula above.

s	-2	3	9
t	28	8	?

What is the missing value indicated by the question mark?

47

Express the year 1066 in Roman numerals.

48

Both the clocks below show times on the same day.

Analogue clock showing a.m. time

What is the difference in the two clock times expressed in minutes?

49

John multiplies 5.6 by 10,000 and then divides the result by 0.2.

What should be John's final answer?

50

The table lists some of the houses for sale at a local estate agent.

Number of houses available	Number of bedrooms	Garage	Garden	Conservatory
7	2	Yes	No	No
12	3	Yes	Yes	Yes
9	1	No	Yes	No
4	4	Yes	Yes	Yes

How many houses have at least two bedrooms, a garden and a conservatory?

END OF TEST

FIRST PAST THE POST

Answer Sheets

Mathematics: Practice Papers

Multiple Choice

Book 2

BLANK PAGE

FIRST PAST THE POST SERIES BY ELEVENPLUSEXAMS

Pupil's Name

School Name

Date of Test / /

MATHEMATICS: TEST A

Answer like this ▬

PUPIL NUMBER

[0]	[0]	[0]	[0]	[0]
[1]	[1]	[1]	[1]	[1]
[2]	[2]	[2]	[2]	[2]
[3]	[3]	[3]	[3]	[3]
[4]	[4]	[4]	[4]	[4]
[5]	[5]	[5]	[5]	[5]
[6]	[6]	[6]	[6]	[6]
[7]	[7]	[7]	[7]	[7]
[8]	[8]	[8]	[8]	[8]
[9]	[9]	[9]	[9]	[9]

EXAM CENTRE

[0]	[0]	[0]	[0]	[0]	[0]
[1]	[1]	[1]	[1]	[1]	[1]
[2]	[2]	[2]	[2]	[2]	[2]
[3]	[3]	[3]	[3]	[3]	[3]
[4]	[4]	[4]	[4]	[4]	[4]
[5]	[5]	[5]	[5]	[5]	[5]
[6]	[6]	[6]	[6]	[6]	[6]
[7]	[7]	[7]	[7]	[7]	[7]
[8]	[8]	[8]	[8]	[8]	[8]
[9]	[9]	[9]	[9]	[9]	[9]

DATE OF BIRTH

Day	Month	Year
[0] [0]	January	2007
[1] [1]	February	2008
[2] [2]	March	2009
[3] [3]	April	2010
[4]	May	2011
[5]	June	2012
[6]	July	2013
[7]	August	2014
[8]	September	2015
[9]	October	2016
	November	2017
	December	2018

1	2	3	4	5	6	7	8	9
117°	84	6.6m³	16	5.6cm	0.1g	A	2	1.53cm
18°	1,771	15m³	86	1.8cm	68.6g	B	5	5.9cm
123°	1,717	2.8m³	82	1.4cm	1,215g	C	6	4.25cm
116°	1,171	10.8m³	83	2.8cm	83.3g	D	4	4.5cm
135°	118	21m³	18	7cm	62.5g	E	3	5.6cm

10	11	12	13	14	15	16	17	18
A	7/9	35	7	(18, 12)	4	25	16cm²	64
B	4/9	841	3	(36, 24)	8	24	28cm²	78
C	1/3	36	102	(24, 36)	5	20	24cm²	168
D	5/9	174	21	(-36, 24)	6	18	8cm²	72
E	2/3	145	5.5	(18, 24)	3	22	32cm²	68

19	20	21	22	23	24	25	26	27
£4.49	(2, 0)	A	2 3/4	50%	-7	469	A	0.99
£5.10	(1, 5)	B	3 1/2	20%	92	491	B	0.0288
£4.40	(4, 0)	C	13/3	14.3%	164	535	C	30
£5.53	(1, 2)	D	3 1/4	40%	432	496	D	24
£4.67	(4, 2)	E	12/3	33.3%	108	415.75	E	32

28	29	30	31	32	33	34	35	36
170	48	4	A	1	26°C	(0, -6)	35cm²	A
106	88	5	B	5	27.75°C	(12, 6)	30cm²	B
265	96	2	C	2	25.25°C	(6, 12)	20cm²	C
212	42	3	D	3	27°C	(-6, 0)	25cm²	D
159	31 7/8	6	E	4	26.5°C	(6, 4)	22cm²	E

37	38	39	40	41	42	43	44	45
27	1,100kg	212	Sat	8	£1.45	9.20	160cm³	A
15	1,050kg	208	Fri	73	£1.25	9.50	50cm³	B
37	1,005kg	206	Mon	41	£1.50	9.19	125cm³	C
91	1,200kg	152	Wed	22	£1.20	9.25	100cm³	D
52	980kg	168	Thu	68	£1.30	9.00	150cm³	E

46	47	48	49	50
18	11	(2, 1)	A	A
16	15	(3, 0)	B	B
14	13	(1, 2)	C	C
12	7	(0, 2)	D	D
10	25	(8, 2)	E	E

BLANK PAGE

FIRST PAST THE POST SERIES BY ELEVENPLUSEXAMS

Pupil's Name

School Name

Date of Test / /

MATHEMATICS: TEST B

Answer like this ▬

PUPIL NUMBER

EXAM CENTRE

DATE OF BIRTH

Day	Month	Year
[0] [0]	January	2007
[1] [1]	February	2008
[2] [2]	March	2009
[3] [3]	April	2010
[4]	May	2011
[5]	June	2012
[6]	July	2013
[7]	August	2014
[8]	September	2015
[9]	October	2016
	November	2017
	December	2018

1
- 10.6m
- 18m
- 11m
- 10.8m
- 1,090cm

2
- A
- B
- C
- D
- E

3
- 591
- 659
- 655
- 595
- 649

4
- 126
- 6
- 7/54
- 7/18
- 42

5
- 120
- 260
- 240
- 200
- 180

6
- 12cm³
- 6cm³
- 8cm³
- 4cm³
- 10cm³

7
- A
- B
- C
- D
- E

8
- A
- B
- C
- D
- E

9
- 26 inches
- 30 inches
- 28 inches
- 34 inches
- 32 inches

10
- A
- E
- C
- I
- D

11
- 7p
- £1.10
- £0.2
- 13p
- 10p

12
- VI
- XI
- VII
- IV
- VIII

13
- 32
- 8
- 24
- 64
- 26

14
- 3
- 8
- 5
- 6
- 4

15
- 25.25
- 25.5
- 26.25
- 26.2
- 25.75

16
- 5
- 11
- 10
- 9
- 8

17
- A
- B
- C
- D
- E

18
- 1/2
- 1/6
- 2/5
- 1/4
- 1/3

19
- A
- B
- C
- D
- E

20
- 4,420mm
- 0.442mm
- 44.2mm
- 4,240mm
- 4,402mm

21
- 60cm²
- 125cm²
- 175cm²
- 225cm²
- 240cm²

22
- 6
- 9
- 7
- 8.5
- 7.5

23
- 800
- 8,100
- 81,000
- 800,000
- 80,000

24
- 50%
- 0%
- 75%
- 25%
- 100%

25
- 4.68
- 50.48
- 50.86
- 4.58
- 631.582

26
- 20
- 12
- 15
- 4
- 13

27
- 6
- 162
- 15
- 33
- 74

28
- 0.19m²
- 0.21m²
- 0.2m²
- 0.17m²
- 0.15m²

29
- (-5, -5)
- (0, 5)
- (-5, 5)
- (0, -5)
- (5, -5)

30
- 162
- 54
- 24
- 18
- 10

31
- A
- B
- C
- D
- E

32
- 1.5 litres
- 2 litres
- 2.5 litres
- 2.25 litres
- 2.55 litres

33
- 37°
- 33°
- 25°
- 28°
- 32°

34
- 2,200cm³
- 2,400cm³
- 2,700cm³
- 2,000cm³
- 2,600cm³

35
- (3, 4)
- (1, 3)
- (3, 3)
- (4, 1)
- (4, 3)

36
- 3/7
- 5/14
- 6/14
- 1/3
- 9/21

37
- 1
- 7
- 13
- 9
- 8

38
- 4
- 8
- 12
- 10
- 6

39
- 99
- 8,352
- 222
- 78
- 126

40
- 26mins
- 14mins
- 16mins
- 24mins
- 22mins

41
- A
- B
- C
- D
- E

42
- 4/9
- 3/5
- 2/3
- 3/4
- 5/9

43
- 39.1
- 35
- 39
- 30
- 40

44
- 38
- 34
- 32
- 36
- 30

45
- 25°C
- 20°C
- 10°C
- 21°C
- 18°C

46
- 32cm
- 48cm
- 26cm
- 28cm
- 20cm

47
- 7
- 245
- 5
- 288
- 42

48
- A
- B
- C
- D
- E

49
- 19.83kg
- 1,983kg
- 1.983kg
- 198.3kg
- 19,830kg

50
- 2,010
- 2,005
- 2,015
- 2,020
- 2,000

BLANK PAGE

FIRST PAST THE POST SERIES BY ELEVENPLUSEXAMS

Pupil's Name

School Name

Date of Test / /

PUPIL NUMBER

EXAM CENTRE

DATE OF BIRTH

Day	Month	Year
[0] [0]	January	2007
[1] [1]	February	2008
[2] [2]	March	2009
[3] [3]	April	2010
[4]	May	2011
[5]	June	2012
[6]	July	2013
[7]	August	2014
[8]	September	2015
[9]	October	2016
	November	2017
	December	2018

MATHEMATICS: TEST C

Answer like this ▬

1
- A
- B
- C
- D
- E

2
- 84kg
- 70kg
- 77kg
- 63kg
- 89kg

3
- 21
- 31
- 5
- 16
- 37

4
- (9, 12)
- (15, 12)
- (3, 12)
- (9, 6)
- (6, 3)

5
- 120°
- 160°
- 100°
- 60°
- 130°

6
- 30%
- 34%
- 25%
- 24%
- 20%

7
- 3
- 2
- 4
- 5
- 1

8
- 2,800cm³
- 7,600cm³
- 7,900cm³
- 7,500cm³
- 8,800cm³

9
- A
- B
- C
- D
- E

10
- 2:1
- 1:2
- 5:1
- 0:6
- 1:1

11
- 18
- 24
- 6
- 12
- 20

12
- 44cm²
- 66cm²
- 52cm²
- 50cm²
- 38cm²

13
- £1.65
- £3.50
- £2.75
- £2.25
- £3.25

14
- 2.4m
- 120mm
- 180mm
- 24cm
- 16cm

15
- 138
- 175
- 226
- 236
- 232

16
- 1
- 2
- 4
- 8
- 6

17
- 117
- 195
- 115
- 193
- 150

18
- (-10, 6)
- (12, -10)
- (-10, 8)
- (8, -10)
- (-10, 12)

19
- 9
- 8
- 3
- 6
- 4

20
- 40%
- 70%
- 80%
- 50%
- 60%

21
- A
- B
- C
- D
- E

22
- A
- B
- C
- D
- E

23
- 9/13
- 3/4
- 9/16
- 7/12
- 2/3

24
- 14.5yd
- 12.8yd
- 7.25yd
- 13yd
- 14.25yd

25
- 4.797
- 4.78
- 4.79
- 4.80
- 5

26
- 6.38pm
- 8.30pm
- 19:30
- 17:30
- 7.30pm

27
- A
- B
- C
- D
- E

28
- A
- B
- C
- D
- E

29
- 87cm
- 1.78m
- 880cm
- 1.83m
- 780mm

30
- 3.8 stone
- 3.5 stone
- 3 stone
- 3.3 stone
- 4 stone

31
- A
- B
- C
- D
- E

32
- 24cm
- 30cm
- 330mm
- 32cm
- 0.03m

33
- NW
- SE
- SW
- NE
- East

34
- A
- B
- C
- D
- E

35
- 294m³
- 333m³
- 334m³
- 343m³
- 284m³

36
- 0.7
- 2/3
- 3/4
- 0.65
- 80%

37
- A
- B
- C
- D
- E

38
- 45 miles
- 70 miles
- 40 miles
- 65 miles
- 35 miles

39
- (1, 4)
- (4, 3)
- (4, 2)
- (0, 4)
- (-1, 4)

40
- £18
- £33
- £48
- £32
- £50

41
- 5°C
- 12°C
- 9°C
- 8°C
- 7°C

42
- 13
- -37
- -13
- -25
- 37

43
- 0
- -0.1
- 0.2
- 0.05
- 0.5

44
- A
- B
- C
- D
- E

45
- 9/7
- 1/14
- 1/7
- 3/10
- 1/21

46
- 1.25gal
- 1gal
- 20gal
- 9gal
- 0.8gal

47
- £2.50
- 65p
- 260p
- £2.20
- £2.75

48
- 278
- 360
- 135
- 556
- 417

49
- £9.50
- £10.25
- £12.67
- £8.75
- £7.60

50
- $p + q$
- $2(p + q)$
- $q + 2p$
- $4p$
- $2p - 2q$

© 2019 ElevenPlusExams.co.uk

BLANK PAGE

FIRST PAST THE POST SERIES BY ELEVENPLUSEXAMS

Pupil's Name

School Name

Date of Test   / /

MATHEMATICS: TEST D

Answer like this ▬

PUPIL NUMBER

EXAM CENTRE

DATE OF BIRTH

Day	Month	Year
[0] [0]	January	2007
[1] [1]	February	2008
[2] [2]	March	2009
[3] [3]	April	2010
[4]	May	2011
[5]	June	2012
[6]	July	2013
[7]	August	2014
[8]	September	2015
[9]	October	2016
	November	2017
	December	2018

1: 20, 80, 120, 32, 40

2: (8, 2), (7, 1), (7, 0), (8, 1), (7, 2)

3: 17.31, 15.71, 17.71, 16.31, 16.71

4: A, B, C, D, E

5: 20, 18, 14, 21, 22

6: Week 1, Week 2, Week 3, Week 4, Week 5

7: 44.4cm, 22.2cm, 6.66cm, 11.1cm, 24.6cm

8: A, B, C, D, E

9: $\frac{1}{3}$, $\frac{1}{2}$, $\frac{1}{4}$, $\frac{1}{8}$, $\frac{1}{6}$

10: £11.75, £12.50, £13.15, £12.15, £12.65

11: 2, 38, 8, 10, 5

12: £357.25, £345.20, £355.25, £357.50, £375.50

13: 03:26, 30:26, 15:26, 3.36, 15.26

14: 5km, 8km, 3km, 6km, 4km

15: 29.9, 29.0, 30, 29.1, 29.09

16: 6, 9, 16, 12, 14

17: 68%, 80%, 72%, 32%, 28%

18: 40mm, 25mm, 10mm, 15mm, 20mm

19: 25, 17.5, 22.5, 16, 27.5

20: 238V, 241V, 238.5V, 239V, 240V

21: A, B, C, D, E

22: 25°, 30°, 36°, 45°, 60°

23: (2, 4), (5, 5), (0, 4), (6, 8), (4, 4)

24: A, B, C, D, E

25: £1.99, £3.01, £2.49, £2.01, £2.51

26: $\frac{2}{3}$, $\frac{1}{2}$, $\frac{1}{6}$, $\frac{5}{6}$, $\frac{1}{4}$

27: 12m, 9m, 10.5m, 6m, 7.5m

28: 130°, 90°, 150°, 120°, 105°

29: 60, 15, 45, 50, 55

30: 64, 80, 72, 48, 68

31: 13, 45, 90, 18, 112

32: 36cm, 32cm, 38cm, 18cm, 34cm

33: 100mm, 76mm, 120mm, 60mm, 80mm

34: (45, 45), (40, 30), (40, 35), (50, 30), (50, 40)

35: 72, 66, 2, 78, 576

36: $7(3n + 4)$, $28n + 3$, $3(7n - 4)$, $28n - 12$, $12n - 21$

37: A, B, C, D, E

38: A, B, C, D, E

39: A, B, C, D, E

40: 4cm², 2cm², 8cm², 6cm², 7cm²

41: Triangle, Kite, Rectangle, Trapezium, Rhombus

42: $1\frac{5}{8}$, $2\frac{1}{16}$, $1\frac{3}{8}$, $2\frac{1}{8}$, $1\frac{7}{8}$

43: 3.15kg, 2.70kg, 12.60kg, 6.30kg, 3.30kg

44: $\frac{1}{4}$, $\frac{2}{5}$, $\frac{1}{3}$, $\frac{3}{8}$, $\frac{1}{7}$

45: 9, 15, 18, 12, 20

46: 16, 56, -8, 2.75, -16

47: LMXVI, MLXIV, MLXVI, LLXVI, LMXXV

48: 300min, 336min, 310min, 333min, 323min

49: 2,800,000, 280,000, 112,000, 56,000, 11,200

50: 12, 19, 16, 11, 21

© 2019 ElevenPlusExams.co.uk — COPYING STRICTLY PROHIBITED

BLANK PAGE

FIRST PAST THE POST

Answers & Explanations

Mathematics: Practice Papers

Multiple Choice

Book 2

TEST A, pages 1 - 8

Question	Answer	Explanation
1	117°	The interior angles in a quadrilateral sum to 360°. d = 360° - (46° + 116° + 81°) = 360° - 243° = **117°**
2	1,717	17 × 101 = 17 × (100 + 1) = (17 × 100) + (17 × 1) = 1,700 + 17 = **1,717**
3	6.6m³	Height of cylindrical section = 5m - (2 × 1.4m) = 5m - 2.8m = 2.2m Volume of cylindrical section = area of circular base × height Volume = 3m² × 2.2m = **6.6m³**
4	83	$\sqrt{4} + 4^0 + 4^2 + 4^3$ = 2 + 1 + 16 + 64 = **83**
5	1.4cm	Radius = Diameter ÷ 2 = 28mm ÷ 2 = 14mm = **1.4cm**.
6	62.5g	Reading across at 2.5oz, the approximate conversion is the halfway point between 50g and 75g, which is $^1/_2$ × (50g + 75g) = $^1/_2$ × 125g = **62.5g**
7	A	Of the 16 letters, 4 letters (I, O, X and Z) have rotational symmetry, which as a percentage is $^4/_{16}$ × 100 = 0.25 × 100 = **25% (= A)**.
8	5	Gemma completed the tasks at the following times: task one at 8.50am, task two at 9.15am, task three at 10.15am, task four at 10.45am, task five at 11.05am and task six at 1.05pm. Therefore, by 11.30am she had fully completed the first **five (5) tasks**.
9	5.9cm	Length of shortest horizontal side = 2.2cm - 1.3cm = 0.9cm Length of longest horizontal side = 2.6cm - 0.9cm = 1.7cm Perimeter = 0.9cm + 1.7cm + (2 × 1.65cm) = 0.9cm + 1.7cm + 3.3cm = **5.9cm**
10	E	The common difference is +37. fourth term = third term + 37 = -17 + 37 = **20 (= E)**
11	$^5/_9$	Five of the nine colours have less than six letters in their names (red, pink, green, blue and grey), which as a fraction is $^5/_9$.
12	174	6 × 29 = **174**
13	3	The mode is the value which occurs with the highest frequency, which is **3** as it occurs three times.
14	(36, 24)	Point F at coordinates **(36, 24)** is directly east of point A at coordinates (18, 24).
15	5	A square-based pyramid has **5** vertices.
16	25	0.375L = 375ml. 375ml ÷ 15ml = **25**.
17	32cm²	The shape covers twelve full triangles and eight half size triangles. Therefore, its area = (12 × 2cm²) + (8 × 1cm²) = **32cm²**.
18	72	$^{75}/_{100}$ × 96 = $^{75}/_{25}$ × 24 = 3 × 24 = **72**
19	£4.49	Total cost = (4 × 18p) + (3 × 9p) + (3 × 70p) + (2 × 70p) = 72p + 27p + 210p + 140p = 449p = **£4.49**
20	(4, 2)	Point P at coordinates (1, 5) is rotated 90° clockwise around point Q (1, 2), taking it to coordinates **(4, 2)**.
21	C	Perimeter = $0.5a + 0.7a + 0.4a + a + 0.4a + a + 0.5a$ = **$4.5a$ (= C)**
22	3 ¼	$1 + ^3/_4 + 1 + ^1/_2 = ^4/_4 + ^3/_4 + ^4/_4 + ^2/_4 = ^{(4+3+4+2)}/_4 = ^{13}/_4$ = **3 ¼**
23	20%	Five of the seven shapes are polygons as polygons have three or more straight sides (the circle and oval are not polygons). Of the five polygons, only one is a quadrilateral (the rectangle), as quadrilaterals have four sides. As a percentage this is $^1/_5$ × 100 = 0.2 × 100 = **20%**.
24	108	Working backwards from the output: ((50 × 4) + 16) ÷ 2 = (200 + 16) ÷ 2 = 216 ÷ 2 = **108**.
25	491	516 - (¼ × 100) = 516 - (0.25 × 100) = 516 - 25 = **491**

TEST A, pages 1 - 8

Question	Answer	Explanation
26	E	The number seven (units column) is ≥ 5, so the number two (tens column) is rounded up to three to give **30 (= E)** to the nearest 10.
27	32	0.96 ÷ 0.03 = 96 ÷ 3 = **32**
28	159	Number of cars = $^6/_2$ × 53 = 3 × 53 = **159**
29	96	second term = first term ÷ 4 Therefore, first term = second term × 4 = 24 × 4 = **96**.
30	4	An acute angle is less than 90°, an obtuse angle is between 90° and 180° and a reflex angle is greater than 180°. **Four** of the six angles are either acute or obtuse (21°, 89°, 91° and 160°).
31	B	$^{60}/_{126}$ = $^{10}/_{21}$. The numerator is 10 and the denominator is **21 (= B)**.
32	3	The temperature was no more than 12°C on **three** of the seven days (12°C on Monday and Friday and 6°C on Wednesday).
33	26°C	The scale goes up in divisions of 0.5°C. The thermometer shows a temperature of two divisions above 25°C, which is equal to 25°C + (2 × 0.5°C) = 25°C + 1°C = **26°C**.
34	(12, 6)	£5 - £2.61 = £2.39, which is shown at coordinates **(12, 6)**.
35	30cm²	Shape consists of a square and triangle. Area of square = 5cm × 5cm = 25cm² Area of triangle = $^1/_2$ × 5cm × 2cm = 5cm² Area of shape = 25cm² + 5cm² = **30cm²**
36	D	When the net is folded up it forms a **triangular prism (= D)**.
37	37	12 + 15 + ? = 27 + ? = 64. Subtract 27 from both sides: ? = 64 - 27 = **37**.
38	1,200kg	14lb ≈ 6kg → 2800lb ≈ (2800lb ÷ 14lb) × 6kg = 200 × 6kg = **1,200kg**
39	212	(19 × 8) + 60 = 152 + 60 = **212**
40	Thu	Monday 14th December minus seven days = Mon 7th Dec. Monday 7th December minus four days = **Thu** 3rd Dec.
41	73	Range = highest value - lowest value = 87 - 14 = **73**
42	£1.20	Total cost of 20 identical pens = £30 - £6 = £24 Cost per pen = £24 ÷ 20 = **£1.20**
43	9.19	The number four (thousandths column) is < 5, so the number nine (hundredths column) remains the same to give **9.19** to the nearest hundredth.
44	150cm³	Volume of cuboid = length × breadth × height Volume = 25cm × 2cm × 3cm = **150cm³**
45	E	240 ÷ 15 = 16 = 4x Divide both sides by 4: x = 16 ÷ 4 = **4 (= E)**
46	14	The full shape consists of **14** corners.
47	11	Prime numbers have only two factors, 1 and number itself. 1 is not a prime number. The first five prime numbers are 2, 3, 5, 7, <u>11</u>. Therefore, the fifth prime number is **11**.
48	(0, 2)	The Town Hall at coordinates (4, 5) is moved three squares down and four squares left to its new coordinates **(0, 2)**.
49	C	Any number multiplied by 0 is 0. Therefore, (2,450 ÷ 12.5) × 0 = **0 (= C)**.
50	B	23 of the 35 squares are empty, which as a fraction is $^{23}/_{35}$ **(= B)**.

TEST B, pages 9 - 16

Question	Answer	Explanation
1	10.8m	As the scale is 1:270, 40mm = 4cm on the map represents a distance of 4cm × 270 = 1,080cm = **10.8m**.
2	B	The lettered points at coordinates (-60, 30), (20, 10), (-60, -30) and (40, -30) are **WNTP (= B)**.
3	659	625 + 34 = **659**
4	42	$7/3 \times 18 = (7 \times 18)/3 = 126/3 = \mathbf{42}$
5	180	Percentage mainly using black pens = 100% - (8% + 32%) = 60% Number mainly using black pens = 60% × 300 = 0.6 × 300 = **180**
6	8cm^3	Number of cuboids making up the whole shape = 15 Volume of each cuboid = 120cm^3 ÷ 15 = **8cm^3**
7	A	The shape has **nine (= A)** faces.
8	D	The time on the clock face is 3.10pm. A quarter of an hour is 15mins. 15 minutes after 3.10pm is **3.25pm (= D)**.
9	28 inches	The waist sizes (in inches) of the group in ascending order are: 26, 26, 26, 28, 28, 28, 28, 28, 28, 28, 28, 30, 30, 30, 32, 32, 34, 34, 34. There are 19 people in total. 19 is an odd number so the median is the 10th value. Therefore, the median is **28 inches**.
10	E	**E** is both directly south of B and directly east of G.
11	13p	Money paid for shopping = £10 + £0.5 + (3 × £0.2) = £11.10 Change on shopping = £11.10 - £10.97 = £0.13 = **13p**
12	VI	Working forwards from the input: ((XX × II) - X) ÷ V = ((20 × 2) - 10) ÷ 5 = (40 - 10) ÷ 5 = 6 = **VI**.
13	8	There are two sequences: odd numbered terms are increasing by two and the even numbered terms are obtained by multiplying the previous even numbered term by two. The next term (9th term) is an odd number. Therefore, 9th term = 7th term + 2 = 6 + 2 = **8**.
14	4	Factors of 42: 1, 2, 3, 6, 7, 14, 21, 42. The bars on the chart have the following values: 3, 8, 1, 5, 1.5, 7, 4, 6. Therefore, **four** of the bars have values which are factors of 42 (1, 3, 6, 7).
15	26.25	210 ÷ 8 = **26.25**
16	10	The regular decagon has **10** lines of symmetry.
17	B	**5 (= B)** sides (vertical lines) are perpendicular to side A.
18	1/3	P(first die shows more than 2) = P(3, 4, 5 or 6) = $4/6 = 2/3$ P(second die shows at least 4) = P(4, 5 or 6) = $3/6 = 1/2$ P(Both occur) = $2/3 \times 1/2 = \mathbf{1/3}$
19	D	Answer **D** shows the cylinder rotated 270° clockwise.
20	4,420mm	4.42m = 442cm = **4,420mm**
21	225cm^2	All sides in a square are equal. Area of square = 15cm × 15cm = **225cm^2**.
22	7	Total points = points for two trapeziums + points for 3 parallelograms + points for 1 triangle + points for 2 hexagons. Therefore, (2 × 4) + (3 × 5) + (1 × 2) + (2 × p) = 25 + 2p = 39. Subtract 25 from both sides: 2p = 39 - 25 = 14. Divide both sides by two: p = 14 ÷ 2 = **7**.
23	80,000	In the number 2<u>8</u>1,902, the underlined 8 is in the 10 thousands column and is therefore worth **80,000**.
24	0%	The test scores are 20, 40, 10, 50. None of the 4 students scored less than 10, which as a percentage is **0%**.
25	4.68	27.58 - 22.9 = **4.68**.
26	15	As 4 out of the 5 cuboids in the pattern are unshaded, the number of repeated patterns required to reach 12 unshaded cuboids = 12 ÷ 4 = 3. Total number of cuboids = 3 × 5 = **15**

TEST B, pages 9 - 16

Question	Answer	Explanation
27	33	Third cube numbed + third triangular number = 27 + 6 = **33**
28	0.15m^2	Area of front of shed = area of triangular top + area of two doors + area of 18 identical panels. 5m^2 = 1m^2 + (2 × 0.65m^2) + (18 × Area of R). 5m^2 = 1m^2 + 1.3m^2 + (18 × Area of R) = 2.3m^2 + (18 × Area of R). 18 × Area of R = 5m^2 - 2.3m^2 = 2.7m^2 Area of R = 2.7m^2 ÷ 18 = **0.15m^2**
29	(5, -5)	Point H at coordinates (5, 5) is rotated 90° clockwise about point (0, 0), taking it to coordinates **(5, -5)**.
30	18	Working backwards from the output, (63 - 9) ÷ 3 = 54 ÷ 3 = **18**.
31	B	Multiples of 6: 6, 12, 18, 24, 30, 36, 42… Multiples of 14: 14, 28, 42… The lowest common multiple (LCM) is **42 (= B)**.
32	2.5 litres	Amount of liquid in top jug = 0.5 litres Amount of liquid in bottom jug = 2 litres Total liquid in both jugs = 0.5 litres + 2 litres = **2.5 litres**
33	33°	The interior angles of a triangle sum to 180°. Interior angles of left triangle are 122° - 90° = 32°, 115° and x°. Therefore, x = 180° - (32° + 115°) = 180° - 147° = **33°**.
34	2,400cm^3	Volume of cuboid = length × width × height = 12cm × 10cm × 20cm = **2,400cm^3**
35	(3, 4)	Point Z is at coordinates **(3, 4)**.
36	$^3/_7$	6 of the 14 rhombuses are shaded, which as a fraction is $^6/_{14}$ = $^3/_7$.
37	9	**Nine** books have more than 90 pages and do not have any pictures.
38	12	The net is of a cube. A cube has **12** edges.
39	126	174 - 48 = **126**
40	24mins	14:10 - 13:46 = **24mins**
41	A	November has 30 days and it rained on 18 of them. As a percentage this is $^{18}/_{30}$ × 100 = $^3/_5$ × 100 = 0.6 × 100 = **60% (= A)**.
42	$^2/_3$	Six of the nine shapes have less than six sides, which as a fraction is $^6/_9$ = $^2/_3$.
43	39	The number zero (tenths column) is < 5, so the number nine (units column) remains the same to give **39** to the nearest whole number.
44	30	1 × 2 × 3 × 5 = **30**
45	20°C	Average = (18°C + 16°C + 22°C + 18°C + 26°C + 16°C + 24°C) ÷ 7 = 140°C ÷ 7 = **20°C**
46	32cm	Diameter of circle = length of rectangle = 2 × 6cm = 12cm Perimeter of rectangle = (2 × 12cm) + (2 × 4cm) = 24cm + 8cm = **32cm**
47	5	$7a$ = 35. Divide both sides by 7: a = 35 ÷ 7 = **5**.
48	E	The direction of the arrow in quadrant Q is given by answer **E**.
49	1,983kg	1 tonne = 1,000kg → 1.983 × 1,000kg = **1,983kg**.
50	2,020	M = 1,000 and X = 10 MMXX = 2 × 1,000 + 2 × 10 = 2,000 + 20 = **2,020**.

TEST C, pages 17 - 24

Question	Answer	Explanation
1	C	72 × 3 = **216 (= C)**
2	77kg	Weight of each smaller brick = $^1/_2$ × 3.5kg = 1.75kg Total weight = (20 × 3.5kg) + (4 × 1.75kg) = 70kg + 7kg = **77kg**
3	37	Common difference is -5. Sixth term = fifth term - 5 = 26 - 5 = 21 Seventh term = sixth term - 5 = 21 - 5 = 16 Sum of sixth and seventh terms = 21 + 16 = **37**
4	(9, 6)	Point J at coordinates **(9, 6)** is directly below point K at (9, 12).
5	120°	y = 180° - ($^1/_2$ × size of one interior angle of the regular hexagon) y = 180° - ($^1/_2$ × 120°) = 180° - 60° = **120°**
6	30%	12 out of 40 people liked both, which as a percentage is $^{12}/_{40}$ × 100 = $^3/_{10}$ × 100 = 0.3 × 100 = **30%**.
7	3	2.58pm + 45 minutes = 3.43pm = 15:43. Only **three** of the five trains would have departed by this time.
8	7,500cm³	Volume = area of end × length = 250cm² × 30cm = **7,500cm³**
9	B	5(x - 4) = 10. Divide both sides by 5. x - 4 = 10 ÷ 5 = 2. Add four to both sides: x = 2 + 4 = **6 (= B)**.
10	1:1	Three of the triangles are acute-angled triangles (i.e. have three acute interior angles), and three of the triangles are obtuse-angled triangles (i.e. have one obtuse interior angle). Therefore, the ratio of acute-angled triangles to obtuse-angled triangles is 3:3 = **1:1**.
11	18	An octagonal prism has 24 edges and a tetrahedron has 6 edges. Therefore, the difference in the number of edges is 24 - 6 = **18**.
12	44cm²	Perimeter of rectangle = (2 × length) + (2 × width) 30cm = (2 × length) + (2 × 4cm) = (2 × length) + 8cm Subtract 8cm from both sides: 2 × length = 30cm - 8cm = 22cm. Divide both sides by 2. length = 22cm ÷ 2 = 11cm. Area of rectangle = length × width = 11cm × 4cm = **44cm²**
13	£2.75	£16.50 ÷ 6 = **£2.75**
14	120mm	The readings on the scales are 16 and 8. The average of these is (16cm + 8cm) ÷ 2 = 24cm ÷ 2 = 12cm = **120mm**.
15	236	Total number of cards in collection = 187 + 49 = **236**
16	4	The shape has an order of rotational symmetry of **4**.
17	117	Numbers between 40 and 70 that are exactly divisible by 13: 52 and 65. Therefore, 52 + 65 = **117**
18	(8, -10)	Following the transformations, the two shapes touch at coordinates **(8, -10)**.
19	3	The mode is 9, which occurs twice. Therefore, two of the three values are known. The range is 6. Therefore, the missing value is either 9 - 6 = 3 or 9 + 6 = 15. The mean is 7, which shows the remaining value must be 3. i.e. mean = sum of numbers ÷ amount of numbers = (3 + 9 + 9) ÷ 3 = 21 ÷ 3 = 7. The smallest number in the dataset is **3**.
20	60%	The first nine square numbers are 1, 4, 9, 16, 25, 36, 49, 64, 81. Six of the ten values inside the shapes are square numbers, which as a percentage is $^6/_{10}$ × 100 = 0.6 × 100 = **60%**.
21	C	$^3/_5$ - $^1/_2$ = $^6/_{10}$ - $^5/_{10}$ = **$^1/_{10}$ (= C)**
22	E	A **vertex (= E)** (corner) is not part of a circle.
23	³/₄	9 of the 12 discs have odd numbers on them, which as a fraction is $^9/_{12}$ = **$^3/_4$**.
24	14.5yd	1 yard = 3 feet → (43.5 feet ÷ 3 feet) × 1 yard = 14.5 × 1 yard = **14.5yd**
25	4.80	The number six (third decimal place) is ≥ 5, so the number nine (second decimal place) is rounded up to 10 to give **4.80** to two decimal places.

TEST C, pages 17 - 24

Question	Answer	Explanation
26	19:30	The time is 7.30pm, which is **19:30** in 24-hour clock format.
27	B	$\sqrt{144}$ = **12 (= B)**
28	E	Working forwards from the input: (39 - 18) ÷ 7 = 21 ÷ 7 = **3 (= E)**.
29	87cm	1.35m - 48cm = 135cm - 48cm = **87cm**
30	4 stone	Weight on scale = 24kg As 1 stone ≈ 6kg → (24kg ÷ 6kg) × 1 stone ≈ 4 × 1 stone ≈ **4 stone**.
31	A	Factors of 68 = 1, 2, 4, 17, 34, 68 Largest prime factor = **17 (= A)**
32	32cm	Perimeter = 6cm + 4cm + 4cm + 4cm + 12cm + 2cm = **32cm**
33	SE	The factory is **southeast (SE)** of the car park.
34	D	The shape is a **cone (= D)**.
35	343m^3	Volume = length × width × height = 7m × 7m × 7m = **343m^3**
36	$^3/_4$	Six of the eight numbers are less than 30. As a fraction this is $^6/_8$ = $^3/_4$.
37	C	The full shape consists of **20 (= C)** corners.
38	45 miles	After 55 minutes the car had travelled halfway between 40 and 50 miles = $^1/_2$ × (40 miles + 50 miles) = $^1/_2$ × 90 miles = **45 miles**.
39	(1, 4)	x-coordinate: (-3 + 5) ÷ 2 = 2 ÷ 2 = 1 y-coordinate: (4 + 4) ÷ 2 = 8 ÷ 2 = 4 Therefore, the coordinates of the midpoint are **(1, 4)**.
40	£50	DVD sale price = 0.8 × £10 = £8 each CD sale price = 0.75 × £8 = £6 each Total price for four DVDs and three CDs = (4 × £8) + (3 × £6) = £32 + £18 = **£50**.
41	9°C	Sum of temperatures: 9°C + 2°C + 12°C + 14°C + 8°C = 45°C. Therefore, the average temperature is 45°C ÷ 5 = **9°C**.
42	37	12 - (-25) = 12 + 25 = **37**
43	0.05	Each term in the sequence is obtained by dividing the previous term by two. Therefore, fifth term = fourth term ÷ 2 = 0.1 ÷ 2 = **0.05**.
44	B	Working backwards from the output: (57 - 18) ÷ 3 = 39 ÷ 3 = **13 (= B)**.
45	$^1/_7$	$^3/_7$ ÷ 3 = $^3/_7$ × $^1/_3$ = $^1/_7$
46	1.25gal	The watering can is holding 5 litres. As 1 gallon ≈ 4 litres → (5 litres ÷ 4 litres) × 1 gallon ≈ 1.25 × 1 gallon ≈ **1.25gal**.
47	260p	Number of 10p coins in the box = (12 × 5) ÷ 3 = 20 Amount of money in the box = (12 × 5p) + (20 × 10p) = 60p + 200p = **260p**
48	556	Number of sides = 139 × 4 = **556**
49	£9.50	£38 ÷ 4 = **£9.50**
50	2($p + q$)	A parallelogram has two pairs of parallel sides, in this case p and q. Perimeter of parallelogram = $p + p + q + q$ = $2p + 2q$ = **2($p + q$)**

TEST D, pages 25 - 32

Question	Answer	Explanation
1	**40**	Multiples of 4 are: 4, 8, 12, 16, 20, 24, 28, 32, 36, 40. Multiples of 5 are: 5, 10, 15, 20, 25, 30, 35, 40. Multiples of 8 are: 8, 16, 24, 32, 40. Lowest common multiple (LCM) = **40**.
2	**(7, 1)**	Point P on triangle T is at coordinates (2, 3) before translation. Translating triangle T down 2 squares brings point P to (2, 1). Translating triangle T right 5 squares brings point P to **(7, 1)**.
3	**16.71**	Using a standard column subtraction method, the difference between the two numbers is 36.28 - 19.57 = **16.71**.
4	**3**	The hexagonal prism has eight faces which is a cube number. The square-based pyramid and the wedge each have five faces which is a prime number. Therefore the answer is **3**.
5	**20**	The prime number sequence shown has the numbers 3 and 17 missing. Therefore, the sum is 3 + 17 = **20**.
6	**Week 4**	Sales match the five day pattern of **week 4**.
7	**22.2cm**	Real length of bridge is 2,220m which is 222,000cm. Length of bridge on drawing = 222,000 ÷ 10,000 = 222 ÷ 10 = **22.2cm**.
8	**12**	The top overlap between blue and green reveals the number of children who like both colours, i.e. **12**.
9	**$\frac{1}{2}$**	Fraction required ÷ $\frac{1}{3}$ = $\frac{3}{2}$. Fraction required = $\frac{3}{2}$ × $\frac{1}{3}$ = $\frac{3}{6}$ = **$\frac{1}{2}$**.
10	**£12.65**	Cost of meal food = £2.50 + £6.00 + £3.00 = £11.50. Service charge = 10% of £11.50 = $\frac{10}{100}$ × £11.50 = £1.15. Total cost = £11.50 + £1.15 = **£12.65**.
11	**8**	Working back from the output and reversing signs gives the equation: Input = ((53 - 18) ÷ 7) + 3 = (35 ÷ 7) + 3 = 5 + 3 = **8**.
12	**£357.50**	TV 2 = 1.3 × £275 = **£357.50**
13	**03:26**	The correct notation is **03:26**. Note the requirement of the zero and the position of the colon between hours and minutes.
14	**4km**	Mean (6km) = (10km + ? + 5km + ? + 7km) ÷ 5. 6km × 5 = 22km + 2(?). 30km - 22km = 2(?). 8km = 2(?). Therefore, ? = 8km ÷ 2 = **4km**.
15	**29.1**	As the eight in the hundredths column is ≥ 5, the zero in the tenths column is increased by one to give **29.1** to the nearest tenth.
16	**12**	Leon's percentage = 100% - (15% + 15% + 20% + 20%) = 100% - 70% = 30%. 30% of 40 counters = $\frac{30}{100}$ × 40 = 3 × 4 = **12**
17	**68%**	Length of plastic tubing before cut = 2.5m = 250cm. Length of plastic tubing left after cut = 250cm - 80cm = 170cm. Percentage of plastic tubing left = $\frac{170}{250}$ × 100 = 17 × 4 = **68%**
18	**20mm**	1.1m = 110cm. Working in cm, total thickness of all five shelves = h - $4g$ = 110cm - (4 × 25cm) = 110cm - 100cm = 10cm. Thickness of each shelf (t) = 10cm ÷ 5 = 2cm = **20mm**.
19	**22.5**	The test results in size order are: 3, 3, 4, 4, 5, 5, 5, 6. Mode (the number that appears most often) is 5. Median (the size order centre number) is (4 + 5) ÷ 2 = 4.5. Product of mode and median = 5 × 4.5 = **22.5**
20	**239V**	Readings: scale 1 = 242V, scale 2 = 237V, scale 3 = 238V. Mean reading = (242V + 237V + 238V) ÷ 3 = 717V ÷ 3 = **239V**.
21	**100**	Cost of all the words = £50 - £30 = £20. Number of words = $\frac{£20}{20p}$ = $\frac{2000p}{20p}$ = **100**.
22	**30°**	As all interior angles of an equilateral triangle are 60°, the six angles along the bottom line of the shape from left to right are: 60°, 60°, 120°, 120°, 60° and 90°. Therefore, angle a = 180° - (60° + 90°) = 180° - 150° = **30°**
23	**(4, 4)**	All y-coordinates on a horizontal line are the same, in this case 4. As any x-coordinate value must be > 3, the only option is **(4, 4)**.
24	**C**	T = 24 + 19n. Subtracting 24 from both sides gives T - 24 = 19n. Dividing both sides by 19 gives n = $\frac{(T - 24)}{19}$, **option C**.
25	**£2.01**	Total cost of potatoes and eggs = £1.29 + £1.70 = £2.99. Change from a £5 note = £5.00 - £2.99 = **£2.01**

TEST D, pages 25 - 32

Question	Answer	Explanation
26	$1/6$	P(tails) = $1/2$. P(5 or 6) = $2/6$ = $1/3$ Total probability = $1/2 × 1/3$ = **$1/6$**
27	9m	Rectangle length = 3m. Rectangle width = 3m ÷ 2 = 1.5m. Perimeter = (2 × 3m) + (2 × 1.5m) = 6m + 3m = **9m**
28	120°	Each ratio part value = $180°/(1+2+6)$ = $180°/9$ = 20° Largest angle = 6 × 20° = **120°**
29	55	Fourth term = $5n$ = 5 × 4 = 20. Seventh term = $5n$ = 5 × 7 = 35. Sum of fourth and seventh terms = 20 + 35 = **55**
30	64	Four box 2 edges can fit across one box 1 edge ($60cm/15cm$ = 4). Number of box 2 that can fit inside box 1 = 4 × 4 × 4 = **64**.
31	90	The product of the prime factors from the factorisation process gives number N. Therefore, N = 2 × 3 × 3 × 5 = **90**.
32	36cm	Number of whole shape sides = 4 (5cm) lines + 4 (4cm) lines. Perimeter = (4 × 5cm) + (4 × 4cm) = 20cm + 16cm = **36cm**.
33	80mm	Cuboid volume (V) = length (L) × width (W) × height (H) $160cm^3$ = L × 5cm × 4cm → $160cm^3$ = L × $20cm^2$. L = $160cm^3$ ÷ $20cm^2$ = 8cm = **80mm**
34	(40, 30)	Coordinates of fourth corner are **(40, 30)**.
35	72	Left column answer = 96 ÷ 8 = 12. Right column answer = 27 - 21 = 6. Bottom row answer A = 12 × 6 = **72**.
36	$28n$ - 12	Output = (input (n) × 7 - 3) × 4 = 4(7n - 3) = **$28n$ - 12**.
37	C	It is likely to rain at least once in **April (= C)**.
38	B	A straight line drawn between two opposite corners splits the pentagon into **a triangle and trapezium (= B)**.
39	A	Statement **A** is untrue as a reflex angle is greater than 180°.
40	$6cm^2$	As triangle CDE is an isosceles triangle, corner E must be midway along AB. Area of T1 = $1/2$ × base × height = $1/2$ × 2cm × 2cm = $2cm^2$. Area of T2 = $1/2$ × base × height = $1/2$ × 4cm × 2cm = $4cm^2$. Area of T1 + T2 = $2cm^2$ + $4cm^2$ = **$6cm^2$**.
41	Rhombus	The shape being described is a **rhombus**.
42	$1\ 5/8$	14 of the 16 sections of the square and 6 of the 8 sections of the circle are shaded. Sum = $14/16$ + $6/8$ = $7/8$ + $6/8$ = $13/8$ = **$1\ 5/8$**.
43	3.15kg	As 1 stone = 14lb, 0.5 stone = 14lb ÷ 2 = 7lb. Parcel weight = 7 × 450g = 3150g = **3.15kg**.
44	$1/3$	Total sold = 15 (red) + 33 (black) + 24 (blue) + 27 (white) = 99 Number of black cars as a fraction = $33/99$ = **$1/3$**
45	15	Ratio part value = 27 ÷ (5 + 4) = 27 ÷ 9 = 3 Number of boys in group = 5 × 3 = **15**
46	-16	The question mark in the table represents a missing t value. From the formula, t = 20 - 4s, when s = 9, t = 20 - (4 × 9), t = 20 - 36 = **-16**
47	MLXVI	1,066 = 1,000 + 60 + 6 = M + LX + VI = **MLXVI**.
48	333min	Analogue clock time is 10.50 a.m. Digital clock time is 16.23 = 4.23 p.m. Time difference is 5 hours 33 minutes = (5 × 60) minutes + 33 minutes = 300min + 33min = **333min**.
49	280,000	5.6 × 10,000 = 56,000 56,000 ÷ 0.2 = 560,000 ÷ 2 = **280,000**
50	16	Houses with at least 2 bedrooms, a garden and conservatory include 12 with 3 bedrooms and 4 with 4 bedrooms. Total number of houses = 12 + 4 = **16**.

Other Titles in the First Past The Post® Series

Mathematics: Dictionary Plus

This book is an indispensable companion to our practice papers and workbooks, containing definitions of key mathematical concepts in accessible language. Each definition is accompanied by a worked, illustrated example and a series of questions to ensure a thorough understanding of its practical applications. The questions have two tiers of difficulty: 'Test yourself' and 'Challenge yourself'. Full answers are included.

This is a comprehensive reference volume, invaluable for all students at 11 plus and Common Entrance exams, Key Stage 2 and beyond.